Write Away

A handbook for YOUNG WRITERS and LEARNERS

Authors

**Dave Kemper, Ruth Nathan,
Patrick Sebranek, Carol Elsholz**

Illustrator Chris Krenzke

WRITE SOURCE®

GREAT SOURCE EDUCATION GROUP
a Houghton Mifflin Company
Wilmington, Massachusetts

Acknowledgements

First, we must thank all the students from across the country who contributed their writing models and ideas. We're also grateful to the many teachers and writers who helped bring *Write Away* to life.

Linda Bradley
Laurie Cooper
Connie Erdman
Gale Hegeman
Michelle Kerkman
Dian Lynch

Amy Nathan
Candyce Norvell
Susan Ohanian
Laura Robb
Charles Temple
Dawn Wenzel-Helnore

In addition, we want to thank our Write Source team for all their help: Laura Bachman, Colleen Belmont, Sherry Gordon, Lois Krenzke, Ellen Leitheusser, Sue Paro, Julie Sebranek, Lester Smith, Jean Varley, Sandy Wagner, and Claire Ziffer.

Page 150 From *Doodle Dandies: Poems That Take Shape* by J. Patrick Lewis. Text copyright © 1998 J. Patrick Lewis. Reprinted with the permission of Atheneum Books for Young Readers, an imprint of Simon & Schuster Children's Publishing Division.

Trademarks and trade names are shown in this book strictly for illustrative purposes and are the property of their respective owners. The authors' references herein should not be regarded as affecting their validity.

International Standard Book Number: 0-669-48234-X (hardcover)
1 2 3 4 5 6 7 8 9 10 -RRDC- 05 04 03 02 01

International Standard Book Number: 0-669-48235-8 (softcover)
1 2 3 4 5 6 7 8 9 10 -RRDC- 05 04 03 02 01

Up, Up, and Away!

The *Write Away* handbook is divided into five parts:

The Process of Writing This part helps you learn all about writing.

The Forms of Writing Here you'll learn how to write letters, reports, stories, and poetry. You'll even learn how to make posters.

The Tools of Learning Reading, word study, and listening are important skills. This part covers them all.

Proofreader's Guide When should you use periods and capital letters? You'll find out here.

Student Almanac This part has facts about science, math, history, and more!

Table of Contents

The Process of Writing

The Forms of Writing

6

The Tools of Learning

Proofreader's Guide

Student Almanac

BOOKS
to Grow In

*There are books to grow in
and books to know in,*

*Books that really please you
and books that sometimes tease you,*

*Books you're glad you found
and books you can't put down,*

*Books with funny pictures
and books that make you richer,*

*Books with a friendly tone—
books you want, all for your own!*

A Book Just for You

Write Away is a book "to grow in." It can also "please you" and "tease you." It is your own friendly book about writing and learning.

Doing Your Best Work

Think of *Write Away* as your special helper. It will help you do your best writing and learning. It is one book you will want, "all for your own!"

All About Writing

Starting to Write

Why are these kids smiling? They know all about writing. They also want to share their ideas with you. To find out what they have to say, read on.

Read, Read, Read

Lindy wrote a story about a little girl and her grandmother. She got the idea after reading Tomie dePaola's *Watch Out for the Chicken Feet in Your Soup.* Here is her advice:

Read a lot of different things. Reading gives you ideas for writing.

Pick Good Ideas

Roger just got his new cat, Henry. He wrote a letter to his aunt telling her all about Henry. Here is his writing tip:

Write about subjects that you really like. Then writing is fun.

Dear Aunt Jenny,
I just got my new cat. His name is Henry.

Try Different Forms

Jenna is always writing something. She writes poems, stories, and notes. She's even writing a riddle book! Here is her advice:

Try different forms of writing. Each one teaches you something new.

Practice, Practice, Practice

Douglas likes to write. He often finds quiet time to write at home. Here is the most important thing he has learned:

To become a good writer, you have to practice. Try to write every day, like me!

Share Your Writing

Ben shares his writing with his friends and family. He likes to see how much they like his stories. He always reads their stories, too. Here is his tip:

Share your stories and poems with others. Sharing helps you write better!

My Poems

Have Fun

Maybe you are just learning to write. Maybe you already write a lot. Either way, follow Kayla's advice:

Using the Writing Process

There are five steps to follow in the writing process.

Think of subjects to write about.

Choose the best idea.

List ideas about your subject.

Write about your subject.

Don't worry about making mistakes.

3 REVISE

Read over your writing.

Check for traits of good writing.

4 CHECK

Check your writing for . . .
* **Spelling**
* **Capital Letters**
* **Punctuation**

5 PUBLISH

Write a neat copy. Share your writing with others.

The Writing Process in Action

Casey wanted to write about her favorite animal. Follow along as she writes her story.

1 PLAN

Casey thought about different animals. She decided to write about Muffy, her dog. First, she listed her ideas about Muffy.

Muffy

Muffy is my dog.

We go skateboarding.

Sometimes Muffy pulls me.

We play hide-and-seek.

Muffy likes to take naps.

She is funny.

2 WRITE

Next, Casey wrote about her ideas. She put the sentences in the best order. This is her first draft.

My Friend Muffy

I like to play with my dog muffy. I sit on the skatebord and tie it. Then Muffy pulls me. When we play hide-and-seek she always finds me. When we race, she always wins. I realy like to watch her sleep and take naps. She falls sometimes when she rolls over.

3 REVISE

Then Casey tried to make her writing better. Here is one idea she added:

> I like to play with my dog
>
> muffy. I sit on the skatebord
>   her leash to
> and tie it. Then Muffy pulls me.
>   ↙←——— added an idea

4 CHECK

Casey also checked her writing for spelling, capital letters, and punctuation. Here are two things she corrected:

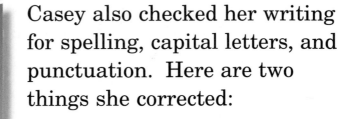

> capital letter   spelling
>
>   I like to play with my dog
>   skateboard ↙
>   M
> muffy. I sit on the ~~skatebord~~
>
> and tie her leash to it. Then

5

PUBLISH

Casey wrote a neat final copy of her story to share.

My Friend Muffy

I like to play with my dog Muffy. I sit on the skateboard and tie her leash to it. Then Muffy pulls me. When we play hide-and-seek, she always finds me. When we race, she always wins. I really like to watch her take naps. When she rolls over, she sometimes falls off the sofa. It is so funny!

 GOOD POINT Later on, Casey may turn her story into a picture book! (See pages 47-49.)

The Traits of Good Writing

People, animals, and things have special features, called traits. For example, a raccoon has the following traits:

- **a black mask around its eyes**
- **little hand-like paws**
- **a furry, striped tail**

Good writing also has special traits:

Interesting Ideas

Clear Order

Personal Voice

Well-Chosen Words

Smooth Sentences

Correct Copy

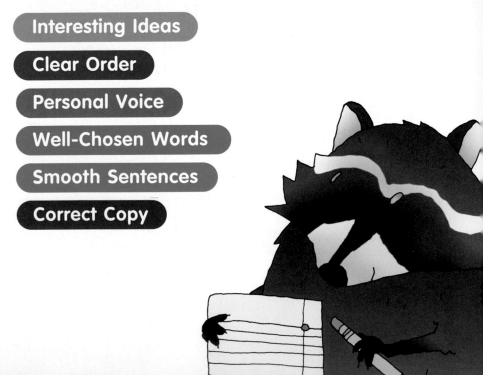

A Closer Look at the Traits

Interesting Ideas

Here is a sentence with interesting ideas. It gets your attention.

While we were swimming, a little burglar visited our picnic table.

Clear Order

This paragraph has clear order. It has a beginning, a middle, and an ending.

While we were swimming, a little burglar visited our picnic table. It was a silly raccoon! I spotted him as I ran back from the beach. He was munching on my jelly sandwich. When he looked up, I think he smiled. Maybe he was saying, "Thanks for the snack."

Personal Voice

Your speaking voice sounds like you, and so should your writing voice. When you use your own words in your own special way, your writing will "sound" just like you. Read the paragraph about the raccoon on page 25. Do you like how the voice sounds?

Well-Chosen Words

There are many words to choose from when you write. Sometimes you need to stop and think of a good word, or change plain words to special words.

Plain words:

He was <u>eating my food</u>.

Special words:

He was <u>munching on my</u> <u>jelly sandwich</u>.

Smooth Sentences

Smooth sentences are fun to read and easy to understand.

Not smooth:

>The raccoon looked up. He smiled. He said, "Thank you."

Smooth:

>**When the raccoon looked up, I think he smiled. Maybe he was saying, "Thanks for the snack!"**

Correct Copy

Writing is ready for sharing when the punctuation, spelling, and other errors have been corrected. You'll find rules for correcting your writing in the yellow pages in this handbook. You'll also find a checklist on the inside back cover.

Prewriting and Drafting

Keeping an Idea Notebook

An **idea notebook** is like a treasure chest full of writing ideas. Ideas for your notebook are all around you. You can write about recess and class trips, families and friends, special places and important happenings!

Notebook Sample

Here is a sample notebook page. Philip used his ideas in a letter to his grandfather.

Philip's Notebook

December 11

I learned to dive!
chin down
bend knees
arms out
fall in
head first

shiver, shiver

Using Your Notebook

You can use the ideas in your notebook when you write. Here's how:

READ your notebook often.

CHOOSE a good subject to write about.

TALK with a partner about your subject.

WRITE about your idea. Try a letter, a poem, a story, or another form of writing.

Jan. 3, 2002

Dear Grandpa,

Guess what? I learned how to dive into the pool. It's fun.

Come and see on Saturday morning.

Love,
Philip

Planning Your Writing

Having a plan helps you to write clearly.

1. Choose an interesting subject.

2. Think about who will read your writing.

3. Gather ideas about your subject.

4. Organize your ideas.

Choosing a Subject

You can write about a subject that you know a lot about. You can also choose a subject that is new to you. Then you can have fun learning all about it.

Gathering Ideas

There are many ways to gather ideas for writing. You can think about what you already know, read books, or explore the Internet. You can also gather ideas by talking to people who know a lot about your subject.

Organizing Ideas

After gathering information, it's time to get organized.

Follow a Plan

- List ideas about your subject. (See page 20.)
- Make a cluster. (See page 234.)
- Draw pictures about your subject.

Choose a Form

- Will you write a poem, a note, a report, a story, or something else?

Writing the First Draft

After planning, write your first draft.

Write the Beginning

One way to begin your first draft is to write your main idea. Here are two ways you could start.

- **I surprised everyone when I went fishing.**
- **My uncle and my dad took me fishing.**

Write the Middle

In the middle, write more details about your subject. Your writing doesn't have to be perfect. The most important thing is to get your ideas down on paper.

**They always go to Eagle Lake.
They think they are the best.
I caught three fish. They didn't
get any.**

Write the Ending

When you write the ending, add one more important idea. Try to give others something to think about.

**They told me I was a good
fisherman.**

Revising and Checking

Revising Your Writing

Edward loves to write. He writes a lot of great stories. Here is one important thing he has learned:

My writing will be good if I make changes to parts I don't like.

Making Changes

Making changes is an important part of the writing process. When you make changes, you are **revising**. You can learn about revising on the next two pages.

Revising TIPS

Follow these tips when you revise:

READ your first draft out loud.

LISTEN to your sentences.

- Are they smooth?
- Are they in the right order?

ASK your teacher or another person to read your first draft, too. Find out if he or she has any questions.

MAKE changes in your writing.

✔ Cross out parts that are not needed.

✔ Change words and sentences that don't sound right.

✔ Add new words or sentences. (You may need to use more details in your writing.)

Checking the Three Main Parts

Make sure your writing has a good beginning, middle, and ending.

Beginning

The beginning should name your subject in an interesting way.

I surprised my uncle and my dad when I went fishing with them.

Middle

The middle should give many details.

They always go to Eagle Lake. They think they are the best fishermen on the lake. I caught three fish. My uncle and my dad didn't catch any.

Ending

The ending should say something important about the subject.

The next day they said I was the best fisherman!

Writing with Partners

Sometimes your teacher, a classmate, or someone else can help you with your writing. Here are three good reasons for writing with a partner:

Planning ● To help you pick a writing subject

Revising ● To help you improve a first draft

Checking ● To help you check your writing for errors

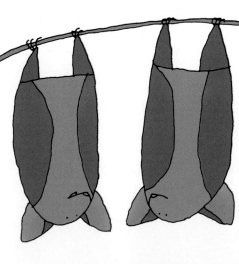

Working Together

What do partners do?

1. They tell you what they like about your writing.
2. Then they ask questions about your writing.
3. They may also tell you ways to make your writing better.

What should the writer do?

1. Listen to what your partner says.
2. Answer any questions.
3. Use your partner's ideas to make your first draft better.

Checking for Errors

Once you have finished your writing— and revised it—it's time to check for errors. Checking for errors is called **proofreading**.

Work Carefully!

It's easy to miss errors, so check your writing very carefully. Use the checklist and tips on the next page to help you proofread.

Proofreading TIPS

READ your writing aloud and listen for errors.

TOUCH each word with your pencil. Underline words that may be misspelled.

FIND a helper. Have your teacher or a partner check your writing, too.

Proofreading Checklist

✔ Did I capitalize the first word in each sentence?

✔ Did I capitalize names?

✔ Did I put a period, a question mark, or an exclamation point after each sentence?

✔ Did I spell the words correctly? (See "Checking Your Spelling," pages 262-267.)

Publishing Your Writing

When you share your writing with others, you are "publishing" your writing. You might read one of your stories to the class. You can also post your writing on a bulletin board or Web site.

Sharing Your Work

This chapter lists many ways to publish. You'll even find ideas for adding pictures and making books.

My Hisss story
by
Sammy Snake

Publishing Ideas

PICTURE BOOKS Illustrate one of your stories to create a picture book.

CLASS BOOKS Put together a book of stories from all your classmates.

DRAMAS Act out stories, poems, or plays.

PUPPET SHOWS Put on a show for your class or for visitors.

GREETING CARDS Design birthday or holiday cards with your own poems and drawings.

CLASS NEWSPAPERS Print your class (or school) news in a class newspaper.

ORAL REPORTS Read or present oral reports for a parent-teacher group.

WEB PAGES Post your best stories or poems on a Web site. (Ask your teacher for help.)

Adding Pictures

It can be fun to draw or find pictures to go with your writing. You can draw them before or after you write.

Drawing One Picture

Auburn wrote a poem about a bird called a quetzal (*say* ket-`säl). After she wrote her poem, she drew a colorful picture.

Quetzal

I am quetzal
living in the canopy.
My tail feathers
are three feet long.
In one day
I can eat
43 kinds of fruit.
My body hovers
like a hummingbird.
I'm an endangered animal.

Drawings in a Picture Book

Sometimes you can make a whole picture book. Jamie made a picture book for his all-about-me story. Each page had one or two sentences and a picture. Here is one of the pages:

I surprised my uncle and my dad when I went fishing with them.

Binding a Book

Book Design

Books can be different shapes and sizes.

Steps to Follow

- Make a front and a back cover.
- Design a title page.
- Stack all the pages between the covers.
- Put your book together with yarn, rings, staples, or string.

Book Cover and Title Page

Sample Cover

Sample Title Page

Sentences and Paragraphs

Writing Sentences

A **sentence** is a group of words that tells a complete idea. Every sentence has a naming part and a telling part.

The Naming Part	The Telling Part
Aunt Jill	laughs.
The boys	play in the yard.

Sentence Parts

Subject

The naming part is usually a noun. It is called the **subject**. The subject names who or what the sentence is about.

Grandpa sings.

Verb

The telling part is called the **verb**. The verb usually tells what the subject is doing.

Grandpa sings.

Other Words

We usually add words to the subject or the verb to make the idea clearer.

Grandpa sings in the shower.

Subject-Verb Agreement

The <u>subject</u> and <u>verb</u> must go together in a sentence.

Singular subjects go with singular verbs.
(Singular means "one.")

<u>Jenny</u> <u>loves</u> milk.

Plural subjects go with plural verbs.
(Plural means "more than one.")

My <u>cousins</u> <u>love</u> juice.

Sentence Problem

Try not to run too many sentences together using the words "and then."

Too many "and then's":

> **José ate his lunch really fast and then he jumped up and then he ran outside.**

Better:

> **José ate his lunch really fast. Then he jumped up and ran outside.**

Writing Longer Sentences

Do you know a way to write longer sentences? You can combine two or three shorter ones.

Two sentences:

Polar bears swim fast.
Polar bears catch fish.

One longer sentence:

**Polar bears swim fast
and catch fish.**

The next page
shows you how to
combine sentences.

Use Two Subjects

Two sentences:

>Foxes live near the North Pole.
>Wolves live near the North Pole.

Longer sentence with two subjects:

>**<u>Foxes</u> and <u>wolves</u> live near the North Pole.**

Use Three Verbs

Three sentences:

>Penguins swim in water.
>They play in water.
>They feed in water.

Longer sentence with three verbs:

>**Penguins <u>swim</u>, <u>play</u>, and <u>feed</u> in water.**

GOOD POINT You can use other words, too.

>**Walruses look <u>sleepy</u>, <u>fat</u>, and <u>wrinkled</u>.**

Writing Paragraphs

When you write, you can describe a subject or give information. You can share a story or give reasons for something. You can do each of these things in a paragraph.

Sharing and Telling

This chapter shows you how to write four different types of paragraphs.

What Is a Paragraph?

A **paragraph** is a group of sentences about the same subject. All paragraphs have a beginning, a middle, and an ending.

Beginning

The first sentence is usually the **topic sentence**. The topic sentence introduces the subject.

Middle

The middle sentences are called the **body**. They tell about the subject.

Ending

The last sentence is called the **closing sentence**. It gives one more idea about the subject.

 GOOD POINT Reading paragraphs helps you write them. You can get started by reading the sample on the next page.

SAMPLE Paragraph – Describing

In this paragraph, Michael describes his favorite sandwich.

My Best Sandwich

Topic Sentence

Toasted cheese sandwiches are great.

Body

They smell buttery and look golden brown. When you bite into one, you can see the melted yellow cheese. Toasted cheese sandwiches taste crunchy on the outside and creamy in the middle.

Closing Sentence

I could eat one every day!

Writing a Describing Paragraph

1 PLAN

Pick a Subject
Pick a person, place, or thing to describe.

Gather Ideas
List ideas. How does your subject look, sound, taste, feel, or smell?

2 WRITE

Write the Three Parts
* Introduce your subject in the topic sentence.
* Give more details in the middle sentences.
* End with a closing idea that's interesting.

3

REVISE

Check Your First Draft

* ✱ Do all of your sentences describe the subject?
* ✱ Does the order of your sentences make sense?

4

CHECK

Check for Errors

* ✔ Check your sentences for punctuation, capital letters, and spelling.
* ✔ Write a neat final copy.

Remember to indent the first line in your paragraph.

SAMPLE Paragraph—Informing

In this paragraph, Kumal gives important information about plants and their roots.

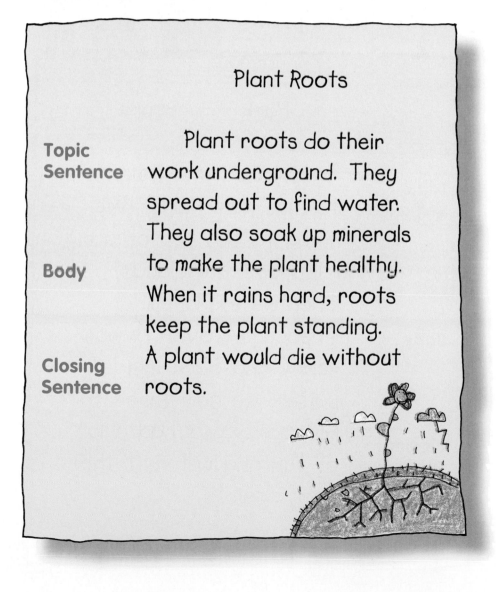

Plant Roots

Topic Sentence

Body

Closing Sentence

Plant roots do their work underground. They spread out to find water. They also soak up minerals to make the plant healthy. When it rains hard, roots keep the plant standing. A plant would die without roots.

SAMPLE Paragraph– Sharing a Story

In this paragraph, Juana shares a story about visiting a park.

Park Adventure

Topic Sentence

My dad and I went to Blue Hills Park. We hiked to the top of a big hill above the clouds!

Body

Then we explored Treasure Cave. It was scary and dark inside. Later, we saw three fat raccoons.

Closing Sentence

We had a lot of fun and will visit the park again!

SAMPLE Paragraph— Persuading Others

In this paragraph, Dee Dee gives reasons for thinking her aunt is special.

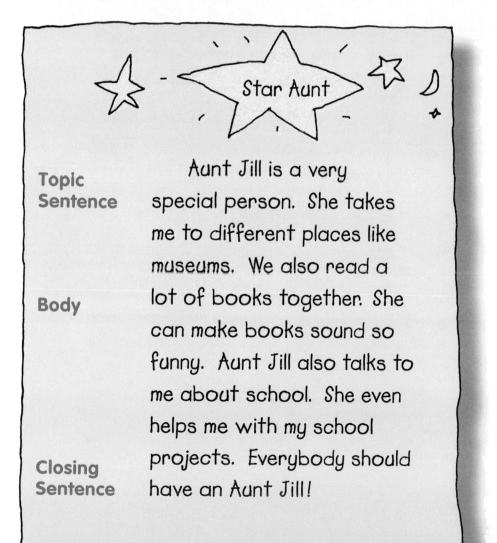

Star Aunt

Topic Sentence

Aunt Jill is a very special person. She takes me to different places like museums. We also read a

Body

lot of books together. She can make books sound so funny. Aunt Jill also talks to me about school. She even helps me with my school

Closing Sentence

projects. Everybody should have an Aunt Jill!

Personal Writing

Writing in Journals

In a **journal**, you can write about how you feel and what you think. It is your very own writing place!

Getting a Present a Day

Josh says, "Writing in a journal is like giving yourself a present every day!" Josh is ready to help you start your own journal. Just follow along.

Journal-Writing TIPS

WRITE in your journal often.

KEEP your eyes and ears open for ideas.

DON'T WORRY about your spelling, but try to write neatly.

DRAW pictures whenever you want to. Drawing can help you think.

READ your journal. You might get good ideas for other writing.

Journal-Writing Ideas

Josh writes about events.

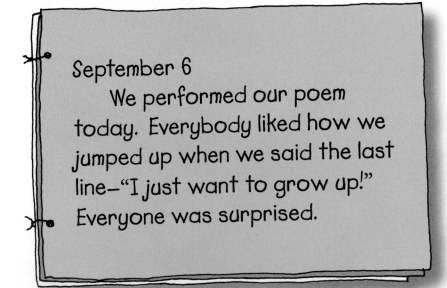

September 6
    We performed our poem today. Everybody liked how we jumped up when we said the last line—"I just want to grow up!" Everyone was surprised.

Josh writes about learning.

January 30
    Here are some good habits
we're learning about in school:
   – eat healthful foods
   – play a lot
   – relax
    Another idea is
to be nice to other kids!

He also writes about his reading.

March 8
    I want to write a book
like Marty Frye, Private Eye.
I'm going to read it again. I
like the silly way Marty finds
lost things. I'm going to make
my mystery funny, too.

Writing Friendly Notes

You can write notes to anyone. You can write to your friends, your mom, or your dad. You can also write notes to your teacher. People like to get friendly notes. It tells them that you care.

Notes Are Easy

To get started, write a note to a friend. Put it in a special place where he or she will find it. You may soon get a note back!

Cool Ideas for Notes

Tell Something You Know

Dear Josie,

An anteater eats 30,000 ants a day. We need one at our house.

Ha ha,
Tanya

Send Good Wishes

Dear Joe,

I'm sorry you broke your leg. We miss you. I hope you'll be back soon.

Your friend,
Eric

Say Thank You

Dear Uncle Mike,

    Thank you for the calculator.
You always know what I need! Now I
can check my math homework.

                Love,
                Sarah

Share a Message

Dear Mom,

Here's a poem for you.
    My mom works hard.
    My mom is true-blue.
    My mom likes to sing,
    And I do, too.

                Love,
                Latisha

Fun Note Ideas

Here are two ways to have fun with notes.

Cut Out a Shape

Lee,
Meet me at the park after school.
Saul

Add a Picture

Linda,
My mom says you can stay over on Friday. We can have pizza. Ask your grandma.

Beth

Writing Friendly Letters

Friendly letters are a lot like friendly notes, but friendly letters travel! They can reach friends and relatives faraway.

Reaching Out

Write a letter and put a smile on someone's face. Jackson did! Read his letter on the next page. Then find out how to write your own letter.

SAMPLE Friendly Letter

Friendly letters have five parts. The parts are marked in this letter.

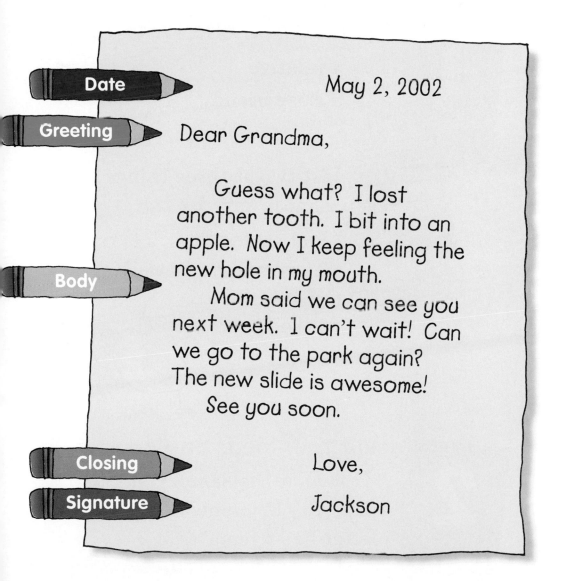

Date

May 2, 2002

Greeting

Dear Grandma,

Body

Guess what? I lost another tooth. I bit into an apple. Now I keep feeling the new hole in my mouth.

Mom said we can see you next week. I can't wait! Can we go to the park again? The new slide is awesome!

See you soon.

Closing

Love,

Signature

Jackson

Writing a Friendly Letter

1 PLAN

Pick Someone to Write To

* a relative
* a close friend

List Ideas

List two or three things you want to say.

I lost my tooth.
We are coming to visit.
Can we go
to the park?

2 WRITE

Put Your Ideas on Paper

Follow the sample on page 73. Remember that a letter has five parts.

Check Your First Draft

3

REVISE

* Did you say all of the important things?

* Did you remember the five parts of a letter?

Check for Errors

4

CHECK

✔ Check your sentences for capital letters.

✔ Check for punctuation and spelling.

✔ Make sure your letter looks nice.

To send your letter, see pages 100-101 for help.

Writing All-About-Me Stories

All-about-me stories tell about things that happen to you. They can be funny or surprising. They can be long or short. They can be old or new.

Getting Started

Read Susan's all-about-me story on the next page. Then turn the page to learn how to write your own story.

SAMPLE All-About-Me Story

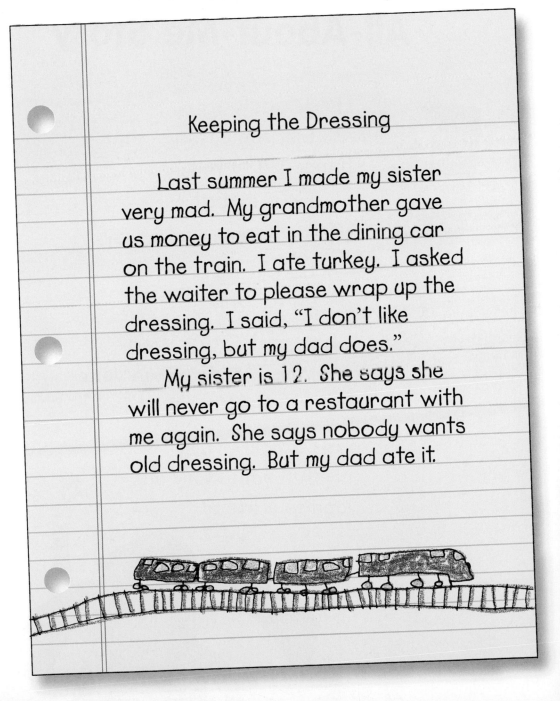

Keeping the Dressing

Last summer I made my sister very mad. My grandmother gave us money to eat in the dining car on the train. I ate turkey. I asked the waiter to please wrap up the dressing. I said, "I don't like dressing, but my dad does."

My sister is 12. She says she will never go to a restaurant with me again. She says nobody wants old dressing. But my dad ate it.

Writing an All-About-Me Story

PLAN

List Ideas

List some things that happened to you.

I lost my cat.

✔ I ate dinner on a train.

I broke my arm on vacation.

Choose a Story Idea

Pick one idea from your list to write about.

Talk About Your Idea

Tell your story out loud to a friend.

Start with a Bang

Here is how Susan began:

"Last summer I made my sister very mad."

Write the Rest of the Story

Tell the details in the middle. Write an ending.

Read Your First Draft

Did you forget anything?

Make Changes

Add any missing parts.

Check for Errors

✔ Check your sentences for end punctuation, capital letters, and spelling.

✔ Write a neat final copy.

Subject Writing

Writing About Books

Reading a good book is fun. Sharing your ideas about the book can be fun, too. You can share your ideas in a book review.

Thinking About Books

This chapter can help you write a book review. It includes two samples for you to read and writing guidelines for you to follow.

SAMPLE Book Review

Here is Jackie's review of a storybook. Each paragraph answers a question.

1. What is the book about?

2. Why do I like this book?

A Very Funny Book

Julius the Baby of the World is a book by Kevin Henkes. This book tells the story of Lilly. She is mad at her baby brother Julius because everybody thinks he is so great. In the end, Lilly changes her feelings about him.

I think this book is very funny. I laughed at Lilly a lot. I think I know how she feels. Sometimes I get mad at my baby brother.

SAMPLE Book Review

Here is a review of an informational book. Each paragraph answers one question.

1. What is the book about?

2. Why do I like this book?

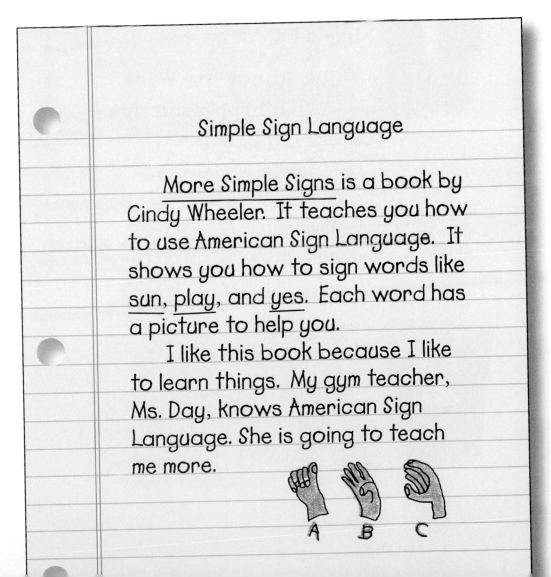

Simple Sign Language

More Simple Signs is a book by Cindy Wheeler. It teaches you how to use American Sign Language. It shows you how to sign words like sun, play, and yes. Each word has a picture to help you.

I like this book because I like to learn things. My gym teacher, Ms. Day, knows American Sign Language. She is going to teach me more.

A   B   C

Writing a Book Review

1 PLAN

Pick a Book

Choose a book that you like a lot.

Think About the Book

What happens in this book? What is the best part? (You could draw a picture.)

2 WRITE

Answer Two Main Questions

* What is the book about?
* Why do I like it?

3 REVISE

Read Your First Draft

* Did you answer the two questions?
* Did you include the most important ideas from the book?

4 CHECK

Check for Errors

✔ Check your sentences for capital letters, punctuation, and spelling.
✔ Then write a neat final copy.

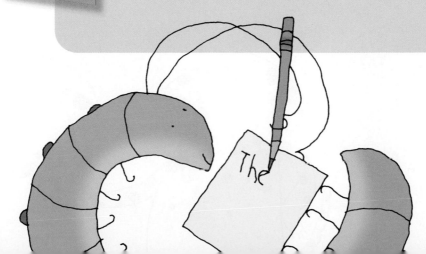

Making Counting Books

Counting jingles are fun to say:

One, two, buckle my shoe.
Three, four, shut the door.
Five, six, pick up sticks. . . .

Counting books are fun to make!

Numbers Plus!

Counting books use numbers (of course). There are special words and pictures to go with the numbers, too.

One spot,
two spots,
old spot,
new spots.

SAMPLE Counting Book

Here is the first page in Shari's counting book called *Circus Fun*. (She counts by 2's.)

Here is the second page in Shari's counting book.

4 Crazy Clowns

 GOOD POINT Shari has chosen words that begin with the same sound (Crazy Clowns). This makes her book fun to read.

Making a Counting Book

PLAN 1

Pick a Number Pattern

* 1, 2, 3, 4, . . .

* 2, 4, 6, 8, . . .

* 5, 10, 15, 20, . . .

Pick a Subject

What will you write and draw about?

Shari picked the circus.

Plan Your Book

What will you write about on each page?

Shari named different circus performers.

Write Your Ideas

* Use special words:
  2 Amazing Acrobats
* Or use sentences:
  Two acrobats did flips.

Draw Your Pictures

Read Your Pages

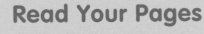

* Do all your numbers fit the pattern?
* Did you use the best words and pictures?

Check for Errors

✔ Look for spelling errors.
✔ Then make a neat final copy of your book to share.

Counting Books That Rhyme

Here's a way you can use numbers and rhyme in your counting book.

1. Make two lists.

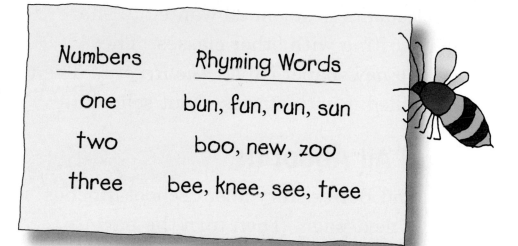

Numbers	Rhyming Words
one	bun, fun, run, sun
two	boo, new, zoo
three	bee, knee, see, tree

2. Write two sentences for each number.

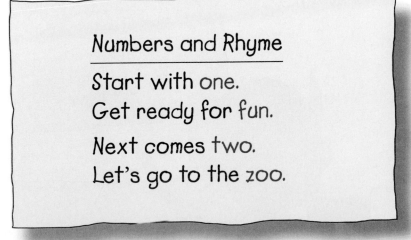

Numbers and Rhyme

Start with one.
Get ready for fun.

Next comes two.
Let's go to the zoo.

Writing News Stories

Students in Room 20 wanted to share their writing with other classes. They made a newspaper called *The Record*. Then they filled it with stories about school life.

Read All About It!

Read Beth's story about school lunches on the next page. Then turn the page to learn how to write your own news story.

SAMPLE News Story

THE RECORD

① New Hot-Lunch Plan

② *by Beth Carmin*

③ This year we have two choices for lunch.

The cooks keep a record of the most **④** popular choices. So far, pizza is the first choice. Hot dogs are the second choice.

Ms. Hunt is our food director. She said, "We **⑤** want students to eat all of their food and enjoy it."

Parts of a News Story

① The **headline** names the story.

② The **byline** tells the author's name.

③ The **beginning** gives the most important idea.

④ The **middle** tells more about the story.

⑤ The **ending** gives the reader an idea to think about.

Writing a News Story

PLAN

List Ideas

List some important events:

our class play

the new lunch plan

Pick One Idea

Choose the best idea for your news story.

Collect Facts

Here are ways to collect facts about your idea:

* Interview people about it.
* Read about it.
* Watch it in action.

Write the Story

2 WRITE

* Give the most important idea in the first sentence.
* Give other facts in the middle.
* End with an interesting idea.

Read the First Draft

3 REVISE

Did you include the important facts?

Check for Errors

4 CHECK

✔ Check your story for spelling, capital letters, and periods.
✔ Write a neat final copy.

Writing Business Letters

Grown-ups write business letters all the time. They send for information. They order things. They try to solve problems.

Sending for Information

On the following pages, you can learn to write business letters, too. Then you can send for information and do other neat things. (Turn to page 170 if you want to send an e-mail message.)

ZOO DIRECTOR
Box 1012
SIMSO IA
53042

US MAIL

Letter-Writing **TIPS**

KNOW why you are writing your letter.

- Do you need information for school?
- Do you want to join a club?
- Do you want to order something?

FIND out who to write to.

STATE your ideas clearly.

SOUND polite and thankful. In most cases, you will be writing to a grown-up.

FOLLOW the form for a business letter and for addressing an envelope. (See pages 98-100.)

USE your best handwriting. (If you can, type your letter on a computer.)

CHECK the letter for errors before sending it.

Six Parts of a Business Letter

1 Heading: Give your address and the date.

2 Inside Address: Write the name and address of the person or company you are writing to.

3 Salutation: Use a title (Officer), or **Ms.** for women and **Mr.** for men.

Dear Officer Friendly:

Dear Ms. Cheng:

4 Body: Explain what you need.

5 Closing: Use **Sincerely** followed by a comma (,).

6 Signature: Write your name under the closing.

SAMPLE Business Letter

1 609 Chicago Street
Baytown, NY 10303
March 30, 2002

2 Officer Friendly
Baytown Police Department
100 Main Street
Baytown, NY 10303

3 Dear Officer Friendly:

My name is Michael Shabani, and I am in second grade. We are going to study bike safety next week.

4 I think you know a lot about bike safety. Please send me your information. It is my job to get information for the class.

Thank you.

5 Sincerely,

6 Michael Shabani

Sending Your Letter

Addressing the Envelope

- The post office prefers that you use all capital letters and no punctuation marks.
- Use the post office abbreviations for states and streets. (See pages 260-261.)
- Put your address in the top left corner.
- Put the stamp in the top right corner.

MICHAEL SHABANI
609 CHICAGO ST
BAYTOWN NY 10303

U.S.

OFFICER FRIENDLY
BAYTOWN POLICE DEPARTMENT
100 MAIN ST
BAYTOWN NY 10303

Folding Your Letter

- Fold your letter into three equal parts.
- Put your letter into the envelope. Then seal the envelope.
- Check the address again.
- Mail your letter!

...and I ...be going to ...ll be next week.

I think you know a lot about bike safety. Please send me your information. It is my job to get information for the class.
Thank you.
Sincerely,

Michael Shabani

How-To Writing

Everyone is good at something. You may be good at hitting a softball . . . or making a delicious peanut butter and jelly sandwich. Yum!

Step-by-Step

In this chapter, you will learn how to write **directions**. Then you can explain how to do something or how to get somewhere.

Two Kinds of Directions

Making a PB & J Sandwich

It's easy to make a peanut butter and jelly sandwich. First, spread peanut butter on one piece of bread. Then, spread jelly on the other piece. Next, put the two pieces of bread together. Keep the peanut butter and jelly on the inside. Last, cut the sandwich in half and start eating!

How to Get to the Nurse's Office

1. Go out of our classroom and turn left.
2. Walk to the stairs and go down.
3. Turn right at the bottom of the stairs.
4. Walk a long way down the hall.
5. Stop at Room 104, the nurse's office.

Writing a Set of Directions

1 PLAN

Pick a Subject

Choose something you like to do. (Or, you can choose a special place to go.)

Think About It

* Who are the directions for?
* What steps will you give in your directions?

2 WRITE

Write the Directions

* Use time words like *first, next,* and *then* to make your directions clear.
* Or, you can write a number before each step.

3 REVISE

Check the Directions
* Did you include all the steps?
* Are the steps in the right order?

4 CHECK

Check for Errors
✔ Check your sentences for spelling, capital letters, and periods.
✔ Then write a neat copy of your directions to share.

You can add pictures to your directions, too.

Making Posters

Posters are like BIG notes. Some posters tell about special events. They tell where and when an event is going to happen. Posters may also say something important about a subject.

Post a Big Note!

Study the posters on the next two pages. Then learn how to make your own.

SAMPLE Poster About an Event

SAMPLE Poster Sharing an Idea

Poster-Making **TIPS**

A good poster needs a lively picture and just a few words. Here are some tips:

GATHER all your facts.

THINK of a main idea for your poster.

PLAN your poster on a small piece of paper.

- Use all the space.
- Write the words in big letters.

SHOW your plan to a classmate. Maybe your friend will give you an idea.

CHECK your spelling and facts.

DRAW your poster on a large piece of paper.

COLOR your poster.

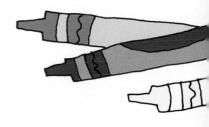

Research Writing

Making Picture Dictionaries

To make a **picture dictionary**, you need to do four things:

1. Choose a subject.

2. Put a set of words in ABC order.

3. Write sentences about each word.

4. Draw a picture for each word.

Picking a Subject

A picture dictionary can be about any subject, from animals to vehicles. You can make a picture dictionary by yourself or with others.

Dictionary-Making TIPS

PICK a subject you really like. Here are some ideas:

> wild animals
> motor vehicles
> healthful foods
> musical instruments

LIST words for your dictionary. Each word should be about the subject.

SELECT the best words. (You don't have to use all of the letters in the alphabet.)

PUT the words in ABC order.

WRITE sentences for each word.

CHECK your words and sentences for spelling errors.

SET UP your dictionary. Each page should have a word, sentences, and a picture.

PUT the pages together and add a cover.

SAMPLE Dictionary Pages

Here are two pages from Room 104's picture dictionary. The subject is vehicles.

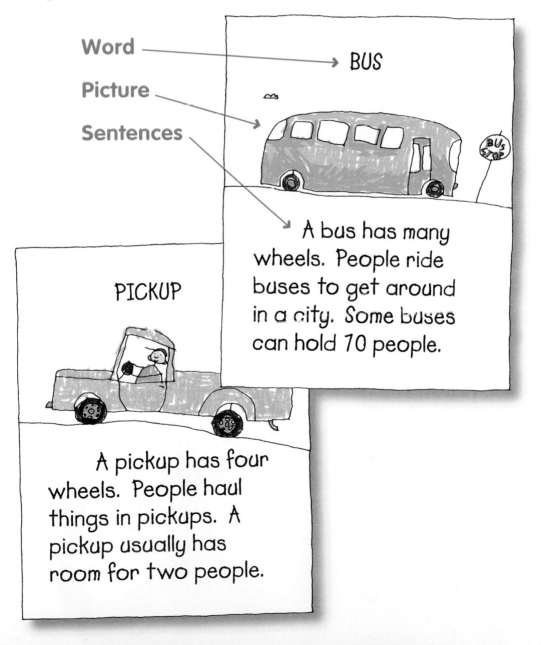

Word → BUS

Picture

Sentences

A bus has many wheels. People ride buses to get around in a city. Some buses can hold 70 people.

PICKUP

A pickup has four wheels. People haul things in pickups. A pickup usually has room for two people.

Writing Reports

John learned three things about his favorite dinosaur: *how big it was, what it ate,* and *where it lived.* Then he wrote a report using this information. You can read his report on page 119.

Finding and Sharing

This chapter shows you how to gather information about a subject. It also shows you how to write a report with your information.

Beginning a Report

Choose a Good Subject

- You can choose a subject you are studying in school.
- You can choose a subject you like to read about. (IIere's the topic John chose.)

  Brachiosaurus

Write Questions About the Subject

- Write three or four questions about your subject. (Here are John's questions.)

  How big was Brachiosaurus?

  What did it eat?

  Where did it live?

Learn About the Subject

- Look in more than one place to learn about your subject. You can check the following sources:

    books, tapes, magazines, interviews, CD's, the Internet

- Think about your questions as you are checking information.

Answer Your Questions

- As you find information about your subject, answer your questions.

- Here are two ways you can answer your questions:

    1. Use note cards. (You will need small cards or pieces of paper.)

    2. Use a gathering grid. (For this you will need a big piece of paper.)

 GOOD POINT If you think of new questions or find other facts, write them on your cards or grid.

SAMPLE Note Card

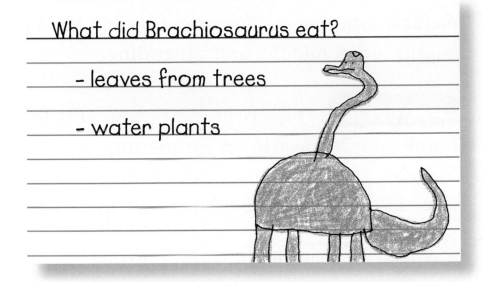

What did Brachiosaurus eat?

- leaves from trees

- water plants

SAMPLE Gathering Grid

Subject: Brachiosaurus	Book	Tape and Picture Set
How big was it?	75–80 ft. long and 40 ft. high	taller than a four-story building
What did it eat?	tree leaves	water plants

Writing a Classroom Report

You can write about your information in a classroom report. Your report must have a beginning, a middle, and an ending.

Beginning   Your first paragraph should name your subject in an interesting way. You can give an important fact or ask a question. (John starts by asking a question.)

Middle   Use the information from your notes to write the main part. Each paragraph can answer one question. (You can also add pictures if you want.)

Ending   Tell what you have learned or how you feel about the subject.

> Remember to check your report for errors before you write a final copy.

SAMPLE Classroom Report

Brachiosaurus
by John Walker

Beginning

What was the longest, tallest, and heaviest dinosaur that ever lived? It was the Brachiosaurus.

Middle

Brachiosaurus was 75-80 feet long and 40 feet high. That is taller than a four-story building! It had a long neck. It could reach the top of 40-foot trees.

Brachiosaurus ate water plants and leaves from trees. It must have eaten a lot. One Brachiosaurus was as heavy as 10 elephants.

Ending

Brachiosaurus lived in the western part of North America. Maybe I'll find a fossil someday since I live in California.

Sample Picture

More Ideas for Reports

This list shows other ways to report on information. You can probably think of many more!

LIST POEM Write a poem that gives facts about your subject. (See the next page.)

STORY Write a story about your subject. (See the next page.)

POSTER Make a poster about your subject. (See pages 106-109.)

PICTURE DICTIONARY Report on your subject in a picture dictionary. (See pages 111-113.)

ORAL REPORT Tell important facts about your subject. Use pictures or examples that show your facts, too. (See pages 230-231.)

SAMPLE List Poem

Garrett lists many facts about an ocelot in his poem.

Ocelot

I am an ocelot.
You can find me climbing
Up the trees
Trying to find my prey.
Some things I eat
Are snakes and lizards.
You can only find me
Doing this at night.
I am four feet long.
My big eyes help me see.

SAMPLE Story

Here is the start of Lauren's story about an otter.

Carl Otter

I, Carl Otter, live in a river. In this river there are hundreds of animals, like snakes, ducks, frogs, fish, salamanders, beavers, and, of course, otters! I love my home . . .

Story Writing

Writing Circle Stories

Jane loves circle stories. A **circle story** begins and ends in the same place. Jane thinks it's fun to figure out how the author will get back to the beginning.

Reading and Writing

One day, Jane's teacher read *If You Give a Mouse a Cookie,* by Laura Joffe Numeroff. After hearing it, Jane had a great idea for a circle story. You can read it on the next page.

SAMPLE Circle Story

If You Give a Kitten Some String!

If you give a kitten some string . . .
She'll play with it.
Then she'll get all tangled up!
Then she'll go in the kitchen so you can
    get her untangled!
Then she'll leave the string there
    because she's tired, and she'll lie on
    your bed.
Then she'll want you to read her a story.
Then the story will get boring, so she'll
    look for some string to play with.
And, most likely, she'll get all tangled up
    again!

 GOOD POINT It could be fun to draw a picture for each main idea in a circle story.

Story-Writing TIPS

READ lots of circle stories. That will help
you write your own. Here are two
books to read:

> *Millions of Cats,* by Wanda Gág
>
> *Rosie's Walk,* by Pat Hutchins

MAKE a map of ideas for your story. Here
is the start of Jane's story map:

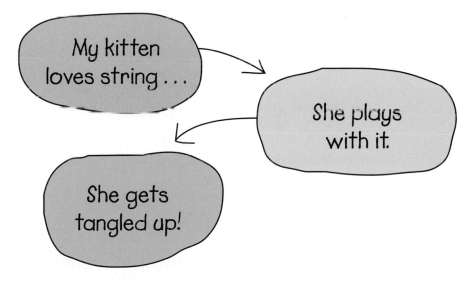

> My kitten loves string . . .
>
> She plays with it.
>
> She gets tangled up!

WRITE your story and draw your pictures.

CHECK your story for errors before you
share it.

Writing Add-On Stories

Stories like "The Very Enormous Turnip" and "Stone Soup" are called add-on stories. Add-on stories are fun to read and fun to write.

The Working Parts

In an **add-on story**, the main character has a problem. One by one, different characters are added to the story. A surprise happens in the end, and the problem is solved.

SAMPLE Add-On Story

Dance Steps

Connie really wanted to tap-dance. She tried, but she couldn't do it.

So she asked Karen, her baby-sitter, to teach her. Karen said, "Sorry, I only know how to line-dance."

Then Connie asked her friend Reba. But Reba said, "Sorry, I only know how to square-dance."

Next, Connie asked her neighbor Mr. Cosford. But he said, "Sorry, I only know how to polka."

Connie thought she would never learn how to tap-dance. Then she asked one last person, her dad. He said, "Sure, I'll teach you how to tap-dance."

So Connie and her dad danced and danced. Everyone was so surprised. No one knew her dad could tap-dance!

Writing an Add-On Story

1

PLAN

Pick a Main Character

In the sample story, Connie is the main character.

List Story Ideas or Problems

Connie's problem is finding someone who can teach her to tap-dance.

List Add-On Characters

Many people are part of Connie's story:

baby-sitter	dad
Mr. Cosford	Reba

2 WRITE

Begin Your Story

Name the main character and tell about a problem.

Keep It Going

Add one character at a time to try to help solve the problem.

3 REVISE

Check Your First Draft

* ✱ Did your characters do fun or interesting things?
* ✱ Did you save a surprise for the end?

4 CHECK

Check for Errors

✔ Check your sentences for errors before you write a final copy.

Writing Fables

A **fable** is a story that teaches a lesson. You may know the fable about the tortoise and the hare. The slow tortoise wins a race because the fast hare stops to rest. In the end, you learn this lesson: *slow but steady wins the race.*

Taking Your Turn

You can write a fable, too. First read the sample on the next page. Then follow the steps in this chapter.

SAMPLE Fable

The Wolf, the Gopher, and the Kid

The kid goat liked to eat in the pasture near his house. He always made sure to leave some grass around the gopher's hole. Gopher told him, "Thanks, that grass hides my hole from hawks."

One day the kid was busy eating in the pasture. He didn't see a wolf sneaking up on him. Then he spotted the wolf and ran toward home. The wolf almost caught the little kid, but suddenly the big wolf stopped. He howled, "Oooww!" His foot was stuck down in a gopher hole. He did not see it.

Safe inside his house, the kid watched the wolf limping away.

Moral: Helping a friend may help you, too.

Writing a Fable

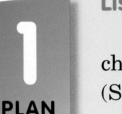

PLAN

List Characters

Pick one or two main characters for your fable. (See the list on the next page.)

Think About the Lesson

Which character will learn a lesson? What will the lesson be? (See the list on the next page for ideas.)

Think About the Setting

Where will your story take place? In a woods? At the beach? In a farmer's field?

Fable Characters

Fable characters are almost always animals. Here are some of the animals found in fables:

donkey	lion	rooster
fox	mouse	sheep
frog	owl	snake
goat	peacock	turtle
horse	rabbit	wolf

Fable Lessons

Here are some lessons often used when writing fables:

- Do not trust someone who only gives you compliments.
- Little friends can be great friends.
- Be prepared.
- Don't count on something until it happens.

2

WRITE

Start Your Fable

Tell where the story takes place. Have your characters meet and talk.

Keep the Fable Going

* Show that one character has a problem or needs to learn a lesson.

* Make something happen. The characters may plan a contest or go someplace.

End Your Fable

Help the readers learn the lesson.

GOOD POINT Use the fable on page 131 as a guide when you write your own fable.

3 REVISE

Read Your Fable Out Loud

Ask a partner to listen for two things:

who the characters are

the lesson in the fable

Make Changes

Rewrite sentences that are not clear. Use your partner's ideas, if they are helpful.

4 CHECK

Check for Errors

✔ Check your fable for spelling, capital letters, and end punctuation.

✔ Then write a neat final copy.

Writing Mysteries

Follow the Clues

Samantha and Josh's whole class wrote mysteries. Read Josh's story starting on the next page. Then learn how to write your own mystery.

SAMPLE Mystery

The Case of the Missing Ring

The main character is named.

Once there was a detective named Josh. He and his friend Ryan went to the library a lot.

In the library, there was a wooden statue. It had a shiny gold ring on its finger. Everyone thought the shiny ring was cool.

One day Josh and Ryan met at the library. Ryan saw that the ring was gone.

The mystery or problem is talked about.

Ryan said, "Look, Josh, no ring. I wonder who took it."

Josh checked for fingerprints. "No fingerprints," he said to Ryan.

→

The main character follows clues.

Then Josh heard a strange sound. He looked to his left and his right. He spotted the library's birdcage. The cage door was open, and the pet crow was gone!

Josh remembered there were no fingerprints on the statue. He knew that crows love shiny things. "I have solved the mystery," he said.

"So, who did it?" asked Ryan.

The mystery is solved.

"Look up there," Josh replied. Just then the crow flew back to her cage. The ring was in her beak!

"I think she's making a nest," said Ryan.

Case closed.

Writing a Mystery Story

1

PLAN

Select a Main Character

List Problems to Solve

Choose One Problem

* Which problem would be the most interesting to solve?

Plan Your Story

* Where will it take place?
* What other characters will be in your story?
* Who will solve the problem?

2 WRITE

Write Your Story

 * Introduce your main character.
 * Tell about the problem.

Keep It Going

 * Put in clues for the main character to follow.
 * Have the characters speak to each other.

Solve the Mystery

 * Help the characters use the clues.

If you get stuck, reread Josh's mystery. See how he put his story together.

Read Your First Draft

Ask yourself two main questions:

Did I put in enough clues?

Did I solve my mystery?

Make Changes

Reword your sentences if they aren't clear and smooth.

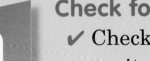 Indent each time someone new speaks. It will make your story easier to read.

Check for Errors

✔ Check your sentences for capital letters, spelling, and quotation marks.

✔ Then write a final copy.

Poetry Writing

Writing Small Poems

The Pool

I live at the pool
in the summer.
The water is green
like a slice of kiwi.
I flip off the diving board—
    SPLASH—
    a belly flop.

Every Word Counts

"The Pool" is a small poem by Clay. Writing a small poem is a fun way to tell about everyday things. When you write a small poem, you can say neat things without using lots of words.

List Poems

There are many kinds of small poems. A list poem is a string of thoughts about one subject. "The Pool" on page 143 is a list poem, and so is Anne's poem "The Wind" below. You can follow the steps on the next three pages to write your own list poem.

SAMPLE List Poem

The Wind

I feel the wind.
It's cold
And wants to brush my face.
I can't see the wind.
It's like having an idea
Hidden in my head.
I know the wind blows seeds
Like dandelions in the summer.

Writing a List Poem

PLAN 1

Think of Poem Ideas

Write down everyday things:

- ✔ wind
- stars
- pebbles
- buses

Choose One Idea

List words and phrases about your idea.

The Wind

- feel it
- brushes my face
- blows seeds

Write Your Poem

Here are some ways to write about your subject:

* List what your subject looks, smells, feels, tastes, or sounds like.
* List what it does, or what you do with it.
* List how you feel about it.

Here are special things to try when you write your poem:

* Use strong action words.
    The wind wants to brush my face.

* Make comparisons.
    It's like having an idea
    Hidden in my head.

* Use pleasing sounds in your poem.
    (Turn to page 159 for ideas.)

Check Your First Draft

3

REVISE

* Read your poem out loud to see how it sounds. Then ask yourself these questions:

  Did I use the best words?

  Did I make special comparisons?

  Does my poem sound like I want it to?

Check for Errors

4

CHECK

✔ Check for spelling, capital letters, and punctuation.

✔ Then write your final copy.

More Small Poems

ABC Poem

An **ABC poem** is one way to use part of the alphabet to make a list poem.

Amazing
Bubbles
Can
Dance
Everywhere.

Diamond Poem

To write a **diamond poem**, follow a syllable pattern. (Lines two and six name the subject.)

bats   (one syllable)
baseball   (two syllables)
pitch hit run   (three syllables)
bases loaded   (four syllables)
first home run   (three syllables)
baseball   (two syllables)
cheers   (one syllable)

Name Poem

A **name poem** is made by using the letters of a name or a word to begin each line.

Cute   Sunny day
Happy   Planting seeds
Red hair   Rain may come
Interesting   Insects buzzing
Silly   Nests with birds
                  Gardening season

Tongue Twisters

Most of the words in a **tongue twister** begin with the same letter or sound. Say the words really fast and feel your tongue twist! Here are two examples:

Crispy crunchy critter crackers crumble.

Tracy teaches tiny tots to tumble.

Making Shape Poems

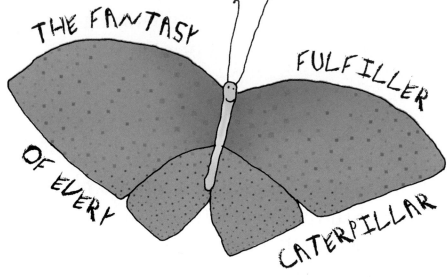

THE BUTTERFLY IS

THE FANTASY

FULFILLER

OF EVERY

CATERPILLAR

Do you like to doodle and draw?

J. Patrick Lewis does! He makes shape poems like the butterfly above. You can, too.

SAMPLE Shape Poem

You can use words to *outline* a shape, as Jaime did.

White cotton balls float by, chased by wind that blows in the sky.

CLOUDS

SAMPLE Shape Poem

You can also pour words *into* a shape to make a shape poem.

My
green balloon
is a toy airplane
without wings. It
floats like a bird in the
sky. A strong wind makes
me and my balloon run
fast and fall to the
ground. POP! The
balloon is pieces of
rubber drifting
to the grass.

Clarke

Making a Shape Poem

1

PLAN

List Shapes

Think of things you like to play with or look at.

football
kite
swing
bubbles

Choose a Shape

Make sure you can draw it.

Collect Ideas for Writing

Clarke thought about his shape, a balloon. Here are some ideas he collected:

green
floats like a bird
in the sky

2 WRITE

Write Your Poem
* Circle your best ideas.
* Put the ideas together into a poem.

Draw Your Shape
Make it big enough for your words.

Put the Poem and Shape Together
Write your poem either inside the shape or around it.

The sun is fun

Read Your First Draft

3 REVISE

* Ask yourself questions:

Do my ideas tell about my shape?

What will others see when they read my poem?

Check for Errors

4 CHECK

✔ Check for spelling, capital letters, and punctuation.

✔ Then make a neat final copy of your poem to share.

Rhyming Poems

Way Down South

Way down South where bananas grow,
A grasshopper stepped on an elephant's toe.
The elephant said, with tears in his eyes,
"Pick on somebody your own size."

Making Rhymes

Rhyming words end with the same sounds. In the silly poem above, the rhyming words are *grow* and *toe, eyes* and *size.* Read about different kinds of rhyming poems in this chapter. Then try writing some of your own poems.

More Rhyming Poems

Couplet

A couplet is a two-line poem that rhymes. First, think of two rhyming words. Then try saying some two-line rhymes using those words. Write down the poem you like best. It's okay if it sounds silly.

Two old forks and a silver spoon
Sit in a drawer and sing a tune.

Where is the rain on a sunny day?
Drip-drop-dripping, far, far away.

Triplet

A triplet is a poem of three lines. All three lines rhyme. Try saying and writing triplets. Begin with a list of rhyming words.

Dana named her dog Tilly.
And Peter named his parrot Lilly.
Now Willy thinks those names are silly!

Quatrain

A quatrain is a four-line poem. Sometimes a quatrain contains two couplets, as in "Who Likes Peas?" Sometimes, as in "Tony's Poem," lines two and four rhyme.

Who Likes Peas?

Birds like seeds,
And bees like weeds.
Mice like cheese,
But who likes peas?

Tony's Poem

I love things that make me laugh,
Like Grandpa's jokes and Dr. Seuss.
I like sunny kinds of food,
Like guava jam and kiwi juice.

Making Pleasing Sounds

Many of the pleasing sounds in poems have special names.

ALLITERATION means repeating the same consonant sound.

Crispy crunchy critter crackers crumble.

ONOMATOPOEIA means using words that imitate sounds.

Drip-drop-dripping, far, far away.

Making Comparisons

SIMILE makes a comparison using "like" or "as."

The water is green **like** a slice of kiwi.

PERSONIFICATION makes a thing seem like a person.

White cotton balls float by, **chased** by the wind . . .

Finding Information

Using the Library

A library is packed with books. There are books about interesting people and places. There are funny books and books full of important information, too.

Looking and Learning

This chapter talks about different kinds of books. It also shows you how to find these books in the library.

Learning About Library Books

Fiction Books

A **fiction book** is make-believe. Much of the story did not really happen. The author made it up.

Look for Them Fiction books have their own place in the library. They are usually found in ABC order by the author's last name.

Nonfiction Books

A **nonfiction book** is true. It contains facts and information. Science books and how-to books are nonfiction.

Look for Them Nonfiction books are put on the shelves in number order. They have "call numbers" printed on them. (See page 166 to learn more.)

Biographies

A **biography** is a book about the life of a well-known person (like a president, an inventor, or an author).

Look for Them Biographies have their own place in the library, too. They are in ABC order by the last name of the person the book is about.

Reference Books

A **reference book** has lots of facts and information. Encyclopedias and dictionaries are reference books.

Look for Them Reference books have a special place in the library. Your teacher or librarian will show you where they are. Many reference books can be found on the Internet.

DICTIONARY

Finding Library Books

Card Catalog

The **card catalog** names the books in your library. A book usually has a title card, a subject card, and an author card in this catalog. All of the cards in the catalog are in ABC order.

Sample Title Card

Call Number   Title   Author

> My Indoor Garden
>
> J 635.9   Lerner, Carol
> LER   My Indoor Garden/Carol Lerner.—New York: Morrow Junior Books, 1999.
>
> Information and guidelines that introduce children to indoor gardening.
>
> Subject ⟶ 1. House Plants

You can look in the card catalog for a title, a subject, or an author. If a title begins with *A, An,* or *The,* look up the next word.

Computer Catalog

Many libraries have their card catalogs on computers. A computer shows you the same information you would find in a card catalog. You just type in a title, an author, or a keyword. A **keyword** works like a subject.

```
Author:      Lerner, Carol
Title:       My Indoor Garden
Published:   Morrow Junior Books, 1999
Subject:     House Plants
Call number:            Status:
J 635.9 LER             Not checked out
Location:
Children's
```

Using Call Numbers

To find a nonfiction book, you need to know the **call number**. *My Indoor Garden* by Carol Lerner has this call number:　J 635.9
　　　　　LER

Below, you can see where this book fits on the shelf.

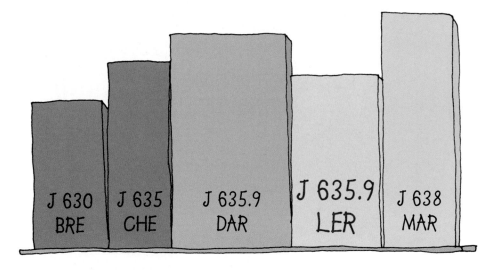

J 630
BRE J 635
CHE J 635.9
DAR J 635.9
LER J 638
MAR

 GOOD POINT Always ask your librarian or teacher for help if you cannot find a book. Either one can help you become "library smart"!

Using Nonfiction Books

Nonfiction books are easier to use when you know their parts. See how many of the following parts are in this handbook.

At the Beginning

- The **title page** is the first page. It gives the book title and the author's name.
- The **table of contents** names each chapter and tells what page it starts on.

In the Middle

- The **body** is the main part of the book. It includes all of the chapters.

At the End

- The **glossary**, if there is one, is like a dictionary. It explains special words.
- The **index** is an ABC list of all the topics in the book. It gives the page number where each topic is found.

Using a Computer

You already know that computers can be very helpful and fun to use. Computers can be used to write, to find information on the Internet, or to send e-mail.

Going On-Line

This chapter can help you use computers for sending e-mail messages and for viewing Web pages.

The Parts of a Computer System

Here are the main parts:

1. The **monitor**
   (shows your work)
2. The **computer**
   (stores information)
3. The **keyboard**
4. The **mouse**
   (moves the cursor)
5. A **disk**
   (saves your work)
6. The **printer**
   (prints your work)

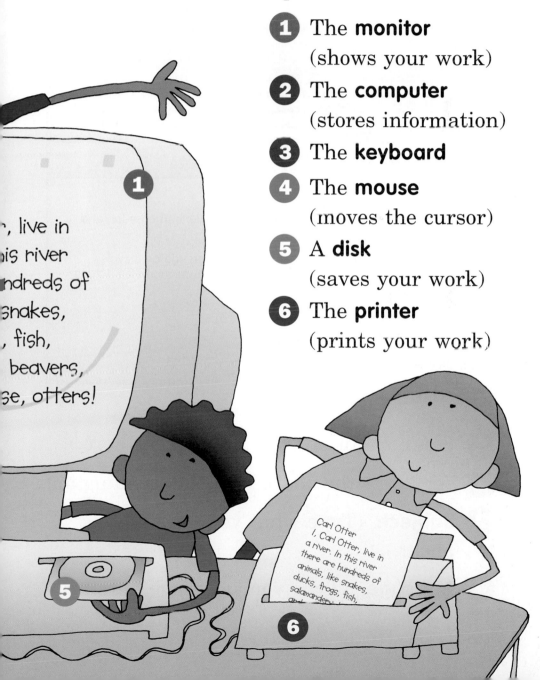

Using E-Mail

You can use a computer to send e-mail.

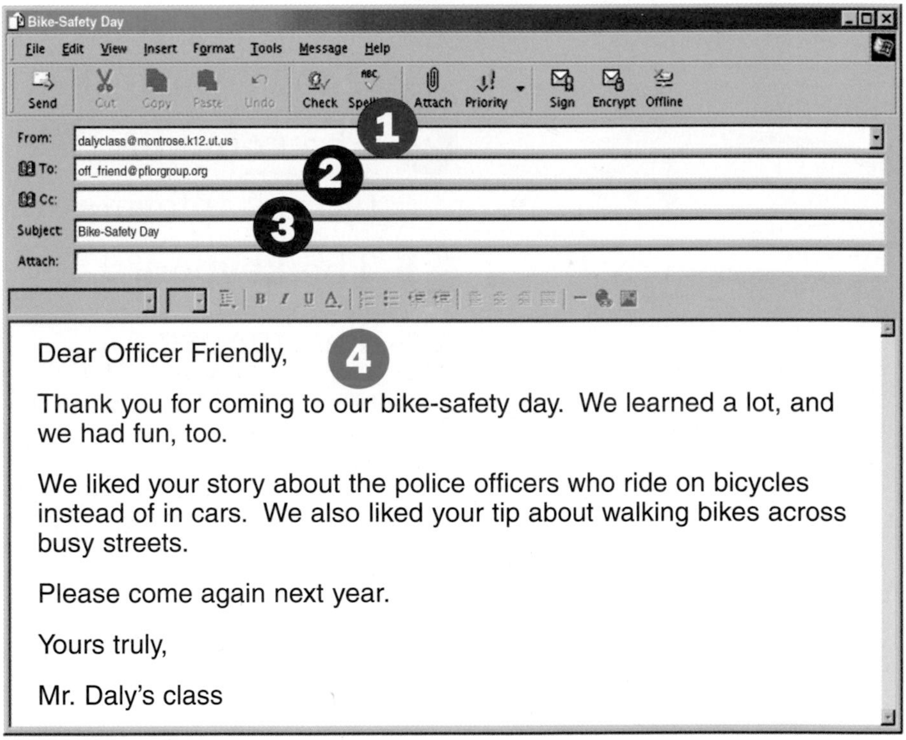

```
Bike-Safety Day                                         _ □ ✕
File  Edit  View  Insert  Format  Tools  Message  Help

 →    ✂      📄     📋     ↺     ✓     ✓ABC    📎    ↓!  ▾    ✉    ✉    ⇲
Send  Cut   Copy  Paste  Undo  Check Spell  Attach Priority  Sign Encrypt Offline

From:    dalyclass@montrose.k12.ut.us                          1
📖 To:   off_friend@pflorgroup.org                    2
📖 Cc:
Subject: Bike-Safety Day                       3
Attach:

        ┌──┐ ┌──┐ E. │ B I U A │ ☰ ☰ ☰ │ ☰ ☰ ☰ ☰ │ − 🔗 🖼

   Dear Officer Friendly,       4

   Thank you for coming to our bike-safety day.  We learned a lot, and
   we had fun, too.

   We liked your story about the police officers who ride on bicycles
   instead of in cars.  We also liked your tip about walking bikes across
   busy streets.

   Please come again next year.

   Yours truly,

   Mr. Daly's class
```

1 **From:** (Your address will appear here.)

2 **To:** (Type the address you are sending to.)

3 **Subject:** (Type what your message is about.)

4 **Message:** (Type your message here.)

Viewing Web Pages

The Web is one part of the Internet. It is made up of "pages." Each page has its own electronic address. When you type a Web address, it moves you to another page. (Try it with <**thewritesource.com**>.)

Parts of a Web Page

1 The **arrows** take you *back* a page or *forward* a page.

2 The **home** button takes you *back* to your starting page.

3 The **address** line shows the address. This is also where you type the address of a new place you want to go.

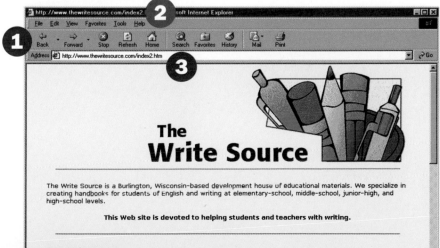

Reading Skills

Reading Graphics

Some pictures are just fun to look at. Other pictures give information. Pictures that give information are called **graphics**.

Picture Perfect

This chapter helps you read four kinds of graphics: **signs, diagrams, tables,** and **bar graphs**.

Reading Signs

A **sign** tells something important.

This sign means "poison."

Mr. Yuk © Children's Hospital of Pittsburgh, PA.
Used with permission.

Clues for Understanding

- Look for letters or words on the sign.

  The RR on this sign stands for "railroad."

- Look for a slash. It means "no" or "not."

  This sign means "no bicycles."

- Look at the color of the sign.

  RED may mean "stop" or "don't."

  YELLOW may mean "be careful."

  GREEN may mean "go."

Reading Diagrams

A **diagram** shows the parts of something or how something moves or changes.

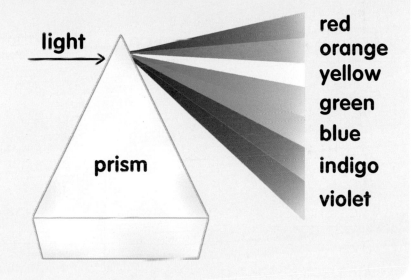

Light Moving Through a Prism

light →

prism

red
orange
yellow
green
blue
indigo
violet

Clues for Understanding

- Look at the whole diagram and then study the parts.
- Read the labels.
- Look at any arrows or pointer lines. They may show how something moves or changes.

Reading Tables

A **table** is a good way to sort things.

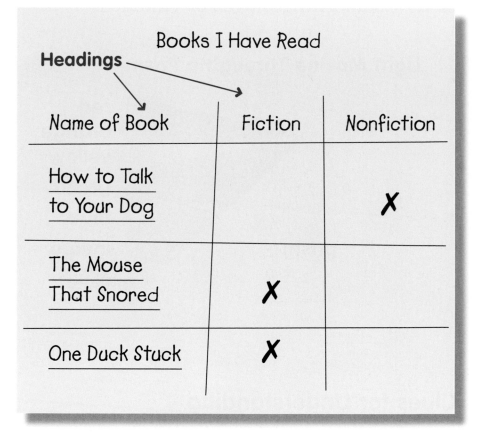

Headings

Books I Have Read

Name of Book	Fiction	Nonfiction
How to Talk to Your Dog		X
The Mouse That Snored	X	
One Duck Stuck	X	

Clues for Understanding

- Read the title to see what the table is about.
- Read the headings.
- Read across each row.

Reading Bar Graphs

A **bar graph** shows how many.

Room 20's Favorite Foods

Number of Students

12	
10	
8	
6	
4	
2	

Pizza   Ice Cream   Candy

Clues for Understanding

- Read the title to see what the graph is about.
- Read the labels at the bottom of the bars.
- Read the scale at the side of the graph. It shows how many.

Reading New Words

There are many ways to read new words. You will find some of them in this chapter.

LISTEN for sounds.

When you come to a word you don't know, you can say the word little by little.

To sound out "map," say . . .

m . . . **mă** . . . **map.**

To sound out "bake," say . . .

b . . . **bā** . . . **bake.**

L⊙⊙K for parts you know.

If you can read the word "oat," you can read . . .

     boat, float, and **goat.**

If you can read "am," you can read . . .

     camp, ramp, and **stamp.**

 GOOD POINT Words like *camp* and *ramp* are in the same family. They have the same vowel and ending letters.

L⊙⊙K for syllables.

Some words are too long to sound out. You need to divide them into **syllables.** Here are two ways to divide words:

Between two of the same consonants

     yel • low   **ap • ple**

Between two different consonants

     pic • ture   **sham • poo**

LOOK for prefixes, suffixes, and base words.

A long word may include the base word plus a prefix, a suffix, or both.

		prefix	base word	suffix
unpack	=	un +	pack	
dishes	=		dish +	es
returning	=	re +	turn +	ing

LOOK for compound words.

Big words may be made up of two smaller words. These big words are called **compound words**.

football = foot + ball

backpack = back + pack

grasshopper = grass + hopper

CHECK for meaning.

After you sound out a word, read the sentence it is in to see if it makes sense. If the sentence doesn't make sense, try again.

- Use the tips in this chapter.
- Think about the other words in the sentence.
- Think about the other sentences on the page.
- Look at the pictures on the page, if there are any.

If you still can't read the word, ask for help.

Reading to Understand

Funny stories make you laugh. Special poems make you feel good. Books with interesting information make you smarter!

Planning to Learn

This chapter can help you read many kinds of books. Each page lists a different plan to help you read, learn, and remember.

WIN Story Reading

Before Reading

- Read the title of the story.
- Look at the pictures.
- Ask yourself this question: What might happen to the characters in this story?

During Reading

- Read part of the story.
- Stop and ask the following questions:
  What is happening to the characters?
  Is this what I thought might happen?
  Now what will happen?
- Read the next part of the story.
  Ask the **WIN** questions after each part.

After Reading

- Think about what happened to the characters.
- Decide if you like the ending.

Preview and Predict

Think about your reading before you start. Then you will be ready to learn! Here is a plan to follow when you read information books.

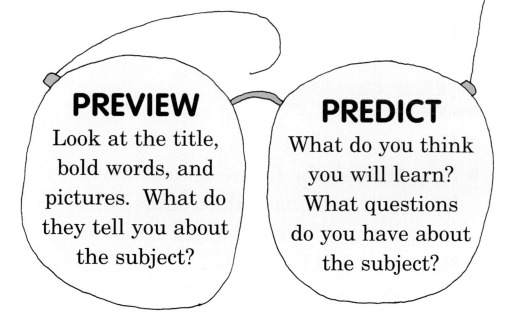

PREVIEW

Look at the title, bold words, and pictures. What do they tell you about the subject?

PREDICT

What do you think you will learn? What questions do you have about the subject?

GOOD POINT Be sure to think about the subject *while* you read, and again *after* you read. Did you find answers to your questions?

Mapping

Mapping, or clustering, helps you keep track of the main ideas in your reading. Here is a map for a book chapter about plants. (The name of the chapter is written in the middle circle.)

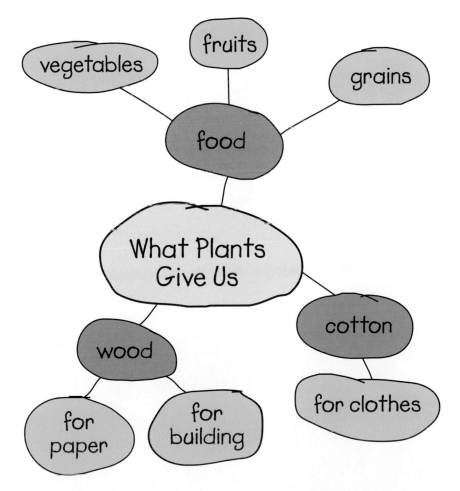

Drawing to Learn

Drawing pictures about your reading is a lot of fun. It shows what you have learned! It also helps you remember what you have learned. Sam read about animal houses. He drew pictures about this topic.

Retelling

Tell a classmate or your teacher about your reading. Talking, or retelling, helps you understand and remember what you have learned. These questions will help you get started:

- What is the most important thing you learned?
- What other things did you learn?
- Are there pictures you'd like to show?

You can do your "retelling" on paper, too. Just write down the things you learned.

Working with Words

Using Phonics

Do you know your consonant and vowel sounds? They can help you learn new words in your reading. They can also help you spell words in your writing.

Sounding Out

This chapter is your guide to phonics. It gives examples of the basic consonant and vowel sounds. Check here when you need help with "sounding out."

Consonant Sounds

butterfly

cup cereal

duck

fish

girl gem

hat

jacket

kite

ladybug

mouse

nest

penguin

quilt

rocket

socks

turtle

vase

wagon

box

yarn

zipper

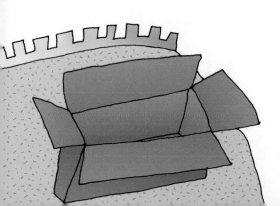

Using Consonant Blends

Consonant blends are two or more consonants that come together. Each letter keeps its own sound. Here are the most common consonant blends:

r blends   brush, cry, drip, frog
grass, pretty, trip

l blends   blue, cloud, flag
glass, play, slide

s blends   skip, smile, snap
spot, star, swing
scrap, spring, straw

ending blends   band, pink, desk
went, must, jump

Using Consonant Digraphs

Consonant digraphs are two consonant letters that come together and have one sound. Here are the basic consonant digraphs:

ch	**chair, lunch, kitchen**
gh	**enough, laughter**
ph	**phone, elephant**
th	**this, thin, bath**
wh	**wheel, what**
ng	**sing, rang, hanger**

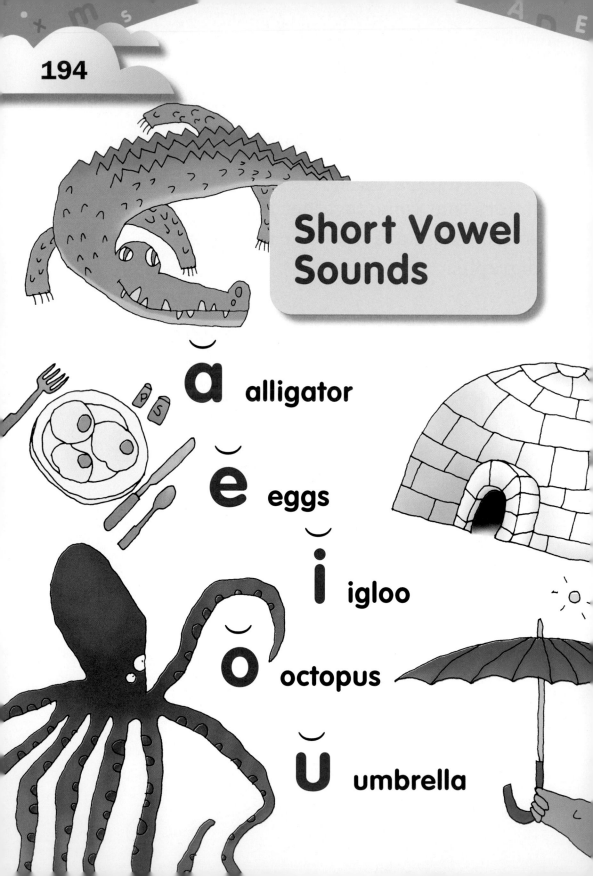

Short Vowel Sounds

ă alligator

ĕ eggs

ĭ igloo

ŏ octopus

ŭ umbrella

Using Short Vowels

Most words with short vowel sounds have this spelling pattern:

consonant - vowel - consonant

short ă	cat	fat	bag
short ĕ	get	bed	men
short ĭ	pin	did	big
short ŏ	hot	pop	fox
short ŭ	rug	bus	fun

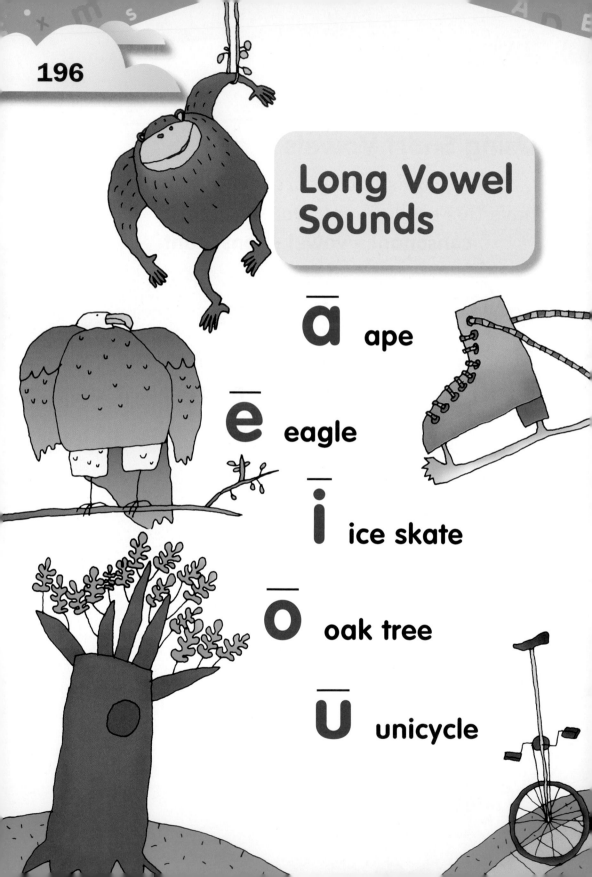

Long Vowel Sounds

ā ape

ē eagle

ī ice skate

ō oak tree

ū unicycle

Using Long Vowels

Words with long vowel sounds have many different spelling patterns.

long ā   game   train   sleigh

long ē   meat   street   Pete

long ī   time   pie   bite   night

long ō   boat   hope   go

long ū   mule   suit   Sue

GOOD POINT Sometimes "y" is a vowel, like at the end of "my," "funny," and "fly."

Using R-Controlled Vowels

Vowels followed by the letter "r" have special sounds.

ar   barn, are, cart

or   fork, more, for

er   fern, person, letter

ir   bird, fir, girl

ur   curl, hurt, burn

The sounds of "er," "ir," and "ur" are the same.

Using Diphthongs

Diphthongs are two vowel sounds that come together. They make a new sound.

oy/oi	**toy, point, coin**
ou/ow	**out, round, cow**
au/aw	**haul, jaw, crawl**
ew	**stew, blew, drew**

GOOD POINT The same diphthong sound can have different spellings.

- You can hear **"ew"** in **stew** and **cool**.
- You can hear **"aw"** in words like **jaw, talk,** and **moth.**

Making New Words

The word "paint" is a base word. You can make "paint" into a new word by adding a word part.

A **prefix** is a part you add to the beginning of a base word.

re + paint = repaint

A **suffix** is a part you add to the end of a base word.

paint + ing = painting

Making New Words with Prefixes

The prefix **re** means "again."

re + build = rebuild

re + tell = retell

re + tie = retie

The prefix **un** means "not."

un + happy = unhappy

un + sure = unsure

un + locked = unlocked

The prefix **tri** means "three."

tri + angle = triangle

tri + cycle = tricycle

tri + color = tricolor

Making New Words with Suffixes

The suffix **ed** means "past."

call + ed = called

play + ed = played

ski + ed = skied

The suffix **er** can mean "a person who does something."

farm + er = farmer

sing + er = singer

teach + er = teacher

The suffix **ing** means "doing or acting."

catch + ing = catching

read + ing = reading

walk + ing = walking

More Prefixes

bi (meaning "two")
bicycle (a two-wheeled vehicle)

ex (meaning "out")
exit (to go out)

sub (meaning "under")
submarine (an underwater ship)

More Suffixes

er (meaning "more")
slow**er** (more slow)

est (meaning "most")
slow**est** (most slow)

ly (meaning "in some way")
slow**ly** (in a slow way)

s, es (meaning "more than one")
balloon**s** (more than one balloon)
box**es** (more than one box)

Making Contractions

A **contraction** is a shortened word made from one or two other words. An apostrophe (') shows that one or more letters are left out.

Waldo doesn't stop playing.

He's a musical monkey!

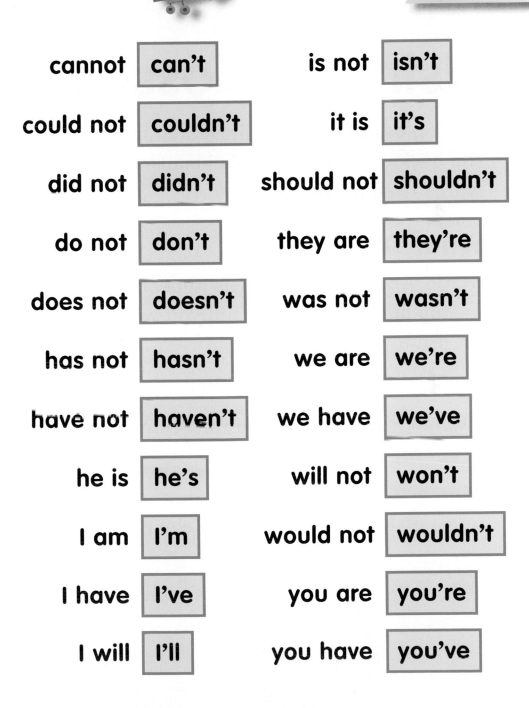

cannot	can't	is not	isn't
could not	couldn't	it is	it's
did not	didn't	should not	shouldn't
do not	don't	they are	they're
does not	doesn't	was not	wasn't
has not	hasn't	we are	we're
have not	haven't	we have	we've
he is	he's	will not	won't
I am	I'm	would not	wouldn't
I have	I've	you are	you're
I will	I'll	you have	you've

Using a Glossary

A **glossary** is like a little dictionary in the back of a book. It tells about special words used in the book.

What You May Find

Guide Words: These words appear at the top of each page and tell you where you are in the alphabet.

Spelling: Each word is spelled correctly.

Meaning: This helps you understand the word.

Sentence: The word is used in a sentence to make its meaning very clear.

Sample Glossary Page

discover ◆ frames ← guide words

D

discover To learn or find out: *I **discover** new things about my baby sister every day.*

duck To lower the head or body quickly: *Kathy **ducked** to keep from getting hit by the ball.*

dune A hill of sand made by the wind: *The children ran down the sand **dunes** at the beach.*

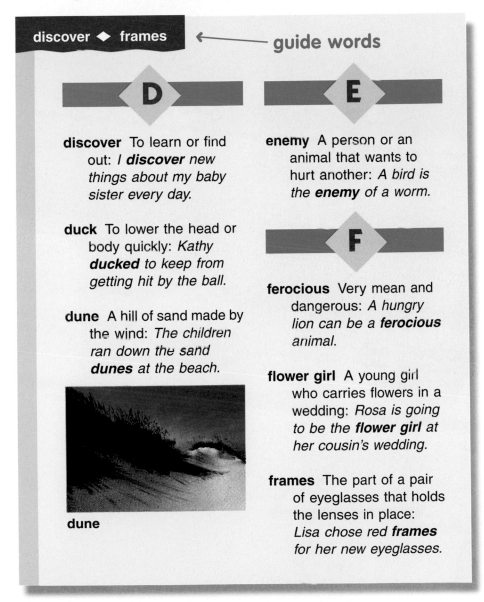

dune

E

enemy A person or an animal that wants to hurt another: *A bird is the **enemy** of a worm.*

F

ferocious Very mean and dangerous: *A hungry lion can be a **ferocious** animal.*

flower girl A young girl who carries flowers in a wedding: *Rosa is going to be the **flower girl** at her cousin's wedding.*

frames The part of a pair of eyeglasses that holds the lenses in place: *Lisa chose red **frames** for her new eyeglasses.*

Speaking and Listening Skills

Learning to View

Most of the time, you watch TV for fun. Programs like **TV specials** help you learn things, too.

Special Shows

TV specials can be about wild animals, planets, dinosaurs, and other interesting subjects. This chapter gives you a plan for watching TV specials, regular programs, and commercials.

Watching to Learn

Before the Special

- **List** your questions about the subject.

  What is a dinosaur?

  How many dinosaurs were there?

  How do we know about them?

During the Special

- **Write** down key words to help you answer your questions.

  What is a dinosaur?
  - a reptile

  How many dinosaurs were there?
  - more than 800 kinds

  How do we know about them?
  - people find fossils
  - experts use computers

After the Special

Here are some things you can do after the program:

- **Think** about your questions. Did you find answers to them?
- **Talk** about the special with someone.
- **Write** about the important ideas.

> ### Dinosaurs
>
> Dinosaurs were reptiles. You can tell dinosaurs by the special way they walked. Their bodies didn't drag on the ground. There were more than 800 kinds of dinosaurs. . . .

GOOD POINT Talking and writing about things help you remember them!

Learning About TV Programs

There are two main types of TV programs. Some programs give **real** reports or show real events. Most other programs are **made-up** stories.

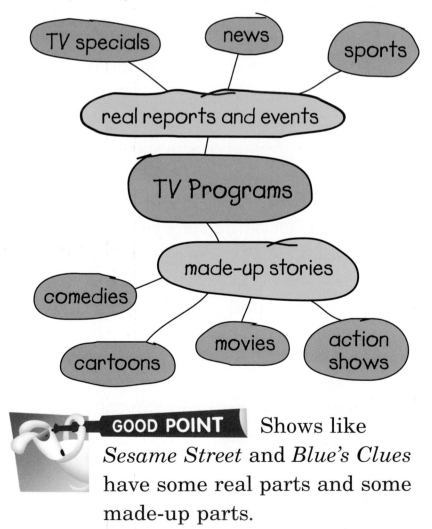

GOOD POINT Shows like *Sesame Street* and *Blue's Clues* have some real parts and some made-up parts.

Learning About Commercials

Most **commercials** try to get you to buy a product. They use bright colors and catchy words to make the product look and sound good. Here are some other things they use:

Famous People

Some commercials show a sports star using a product. If Sammy drinks Sun Soda, it must be good! (Is this always true?)

Groups of People

A commercial may show many kids eating a new candy bar. Other kids may want to join the group and eat one, too!

Problem Solving

Some commercials show a product solving a problem. Maybe new soccer shoes help a player do better. So they must be good! (Is this always true?)

Learning to Listen

It's a good thing you have two ears. You need them for holding your sunglasses or for wearing earrings. Mostly you need them for listening.

Tuning In

Listening is a great way to learn. You listen to your parents, your teachers, and your friends. The next page will show you how to be a good listener.

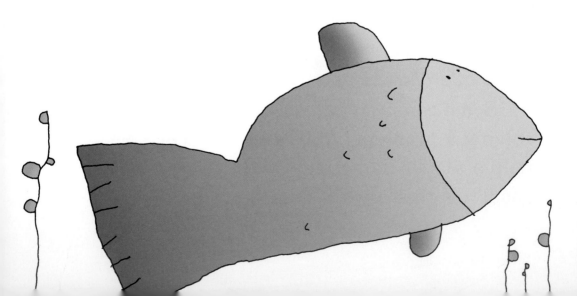

How to Be a Good Listener

Look at the person who is speaking. This helps you pay attention.

Listen for key words. They help you remember important facts.

> **The Pacific Ocean is the biggest ocean.**
>
> **The Arctic Ocean is the smallest ocean.**

Listen for directions. They tell you what to do.

> **Read about quetzals on page 46. List the new words you find.**

Ask questions. When you don't understand something, ask for help.

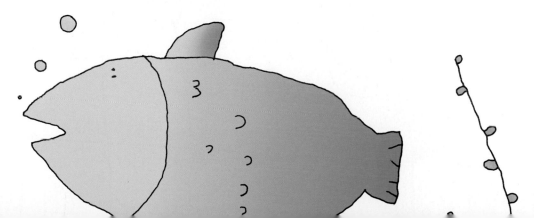

Learning to Interview

Interviewing is a fun way to learn. In an **interview**, you ask someone questions. The person answers the questions. This chapter shows you how to interview.

Talking with a Doctor

Cheryl interviewed Jennifer Miller. Dr. Miller is a vet (animal doctor) who is deaf. Read Cheryl's interview at the end of this chapter to find out what she learned.

Before the Interview

- **Write** questions to ask the person. Think of questions that begin with **why, how,** and **what**.

  > Why did you become a vet?
  >
  > How did you learn in school?
  >
  > What do you like best about being a vet?

- **Set up** a time and place to meet for the interview.

- **Gather** your supplies. You need your list of questions and two sharp pencils.

During the Interview

- **Introduce** yourself.
- **Ask** your questions one at a time.
- **Listen** carefully to the answers.
- **Take** notes.

Why did you become a vet?

I always loved animals.

I played with stuffed animals.

How did you learn in school?

- **Thank** the person at the end of the interview.

Thank you.

After the Interview

● **Share** what you have learned.

Here is Cheryl's report from her interview.

My Interview with a Vet

Jennifer Miller is a veterinarian. She is also deaf.

Dr. Miller always loved animals. When she was little, she played with stuffed animals. It was hard for Dr. Miller to learn in school. Sometimes friends took notes for her.

Are you wondering how Dr. Miller answered my questions? She can read lips. She can also talk. I really liked interviewing Dr. Miller.

Performing Stories

Have you ever wanted to perform a story? That's just what Kasey and her friends did. They read one of her stories in a reader's theater performance.

Reader's Theater

In reader's theater, you don't have to learn the lines by heart. You read them! This chapter shows you how to plan and perform a story in this special way.

Meow!

Planning to Perform

 Pick a Story ● Choose a story with characters who talk to one another a lot.

 Form a Team ● You need a reader for each character. You also need a narrator to read the nonspeaking parts.

 Mark the Speaking Parts ● Mark what each character and the narrator will say. You could also write the story in script form. (See the next two pages for help.)

 Practice Your Reading
● Decide who gets which part.
● Plan where to sit or stand.
● Practice the reading.

SAMPLE Story

Here is the first part of Kasey's story. On the next page, you will see her script.

The Yellow Elephant: Part 1

Once upon a time, Elmer went fishing by himself. His mom and dad said, "Don't talk to yellow elephants."

Elmer said, "OK!"

He went to his best fishing spot. He was so excited because he caught 10 fish. Then it was time to go home. On the way, he saw a yellow elephant.

The elephant said, "Hello!"

Elmer said, "My mom and dad told me not to talk to yellow elephants!"

"But I'm lost," said the elephant.

Elmer thought, "I better run home."

Elmer headed for home, and the elephant followed close behind.

SAMPLE Script

The Yellow Elephant: Part 1

NARRATOR: Once upon a time, Elmer went fishing by himself.

MOM AND DAD: Don't talk to yellow elephants.

ELMER: OK, I won't.

NARRATOR: Elmer went to his best fishing spot.

ELMER: Wow! I caught 10 fish! Now it's time to go home.

NARRATOR: On the way home, Elmer saw a yellow elephant.

ELEPHANT: Hello!

ELMER: My mom and dad told me not to talk to yellow elephants!

ELEPHANT: But I'm lost.

ELMER: (thinking out loud) I better run home.

NARRATOR: Elmer headed for home, and the elephant followed him.

TIP
To make a script, you may need to drop or change some words in the story.

Performing  TIPS

Follow these tips when you are ready to perform your story:

INTRODUCE the story.

LOOK up from time to time when reading.

- Characters should look at the person they are talking to.
- The narrator should look at the audience.

USE your best outside voice.

KEEP going if someone makes a mistake.

JOIN hands and bow together at the end of the performance.

Remember: Costumes are fun. Try to keep them simple.

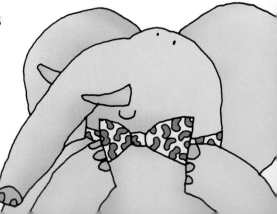

Next Step

Here is the second part of Kasey's story. Try writing a script for this part. Then practice and perform the whole story!

The Yellow Elephant: Part 2

"Mom! Dad!" yelled Elmer. "A yellow elephant is following me!"

His mom and dad said, "Send him back where he came from. He is dangerous."

"No, he isn't," said Elmer.

"Send him back," said his mom and dad.

Elmer sent him back. By then it was time to go to bed.

In the morning, he heard something. He looked outside. There was a yellow bird in a cage. He went outside and got it.

The bird whispered to him, "I am the yellow elephant," and Elmer believed him.

He asked his mom and dad if he could keep the bird, and they said, "Yes."

So he hung the cage up in his room, and everyone was happy.

Telling Stories

Sometimes you hear a story that is so good, you want to tell it to your friends. Folktales and fairy tales can be like that.

Once Upon a Time . . .

This chapter helps you tell stories. First read the folktale "The Three Billy Goats Gruff." (You can use this story for practice.) Then learn some great storytelling tips.

SAMPLE Story

The Three Billy Goats Gruff

Once upon a time, there were three billy goats named Gruff. They wanted to go up to the hillside to eat, but they had to cross a bridge to get there. Under this bridge, lived a great, ugly troll.

The youngest Billy Goat Gruff was the first to cross the bridge. *Trip, trap! Trip, trap!*

"Who's that trip-trapping over my bridge?" yelled the troll.

"It is I, the youngest Billy Goat Gruff. I am going up to the hillside to eat," said the scared little billy goat.

"Well, I'm going to gobble you up!" said the troll.

"Don't eat me. I'm too little," said the billy goat. "Wait for the second Billy Goat Gruff. He's bigger."

"Very well," said the troll.

Then the second Billy Goat Gruff walked across the bridge. *Trip, trap! Trip, trap! Trip, trap!*

"Who's that trip-trapping over my bridge?" yelled the troll.

"It is I, the second Billy Goat Gruff. I am going up to the hillside to eat."

"Well, I'm going to gobble you up!" said the troll.

"Don't eat me. I'm not big enough," said the billy goat. "Wait for the oldest Billy Goat Gruff. He's much bigger."

"Very well," said the troll.

Just then the oldest Billy Goat Gruff walked across the bridge. ***Trip, trap! Trip, trap! Trip, trap! Trip, trap!*** He was very, very big.

"Who's that trip-trapping over my bridge?" yelled the troll.

"It is I, the oldest Billy Goat Gruff!" said the brave billy goat in a loud voice.

"Well, I'm going to gobble you up!" yelled the troll.

"Well, come along then! I'm not afraid of you!" said the big Billy Goat Gruff.

Up rushed the troll, and the big Billy Goat Gruff took care of him in no time! After that, the oldest billy goat went up to the hillside with his younger brothers.

There the three billy goats got so fat, they were hardly able to walk home again.

So . . . **snip, snap, snout,** this tale's told out.

Storytelling TIPS

CHOOSE a story you really like—one that is not too long.

WRITE down the first and the last lines on different note cards. (Half sheets of paper work, too.) This way, you can read the beginning and the ending if you want to.

PRACTICE telling your story. Picture it in your head as you go along.

MAKE more note cards if you need them. Write down short clues to help you remember the main story parts.

USE your best voice. Add special feeling to important lines. (Don't talk too fast.)

TELL your story to your classmates or your family.

Giving Oral Reports

Do you have a collection? Do you know how to make something? Have you just read about an interesting subject?

Telling and Showing

You can share your special information in an oral report. An **oral report** is part *telling* and part *showing*. You tell important facts about your subject, and you show pictures to go with them.

Planning Your Report

In the **beginning** . . .

- Name your subject in an interesting way.

In the **middle** . . .

- Give some main facts about your subject.
- Have pictures, charts, or examples to show.

In the **end** . . .

- Tell why this subject is important for you, or for others.

 GOOD POINT To help you remember things, list your main ideas on note cards.

Giving Your Report

- **Use** your best outside voice. (Don't speak too fast!)
- **Look** at your classmates.
- **Try** to stand still.

Learning and Thinking Skills

Using Graphic Organizers

To play a board game, you have to get organized. You must get out all the pieces, and set them up in the right way.

Thinking on Paper

When you think about an important subject, you have to get organized, too. This chapter shows you how.

Clustering

A **cluster** helps you remember details about a subject or a story. Write your subject in the middle of your paper. Circle it. Then write the details around your subject.

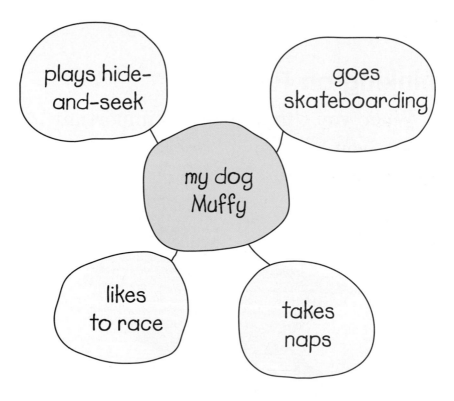

plays hide-and-seek

goes skateboarding

my dog Muffy

likes to race

takes naps

TIP This cluster goes with the story, "My Friend Muffy," on page 23.

Describing a Subject

A **describing wheel** helps you collect details about a subject. Write your subject in the middle of the wheel. Write your describing words between the spokes.

Describing words can be things you see, hear, feel, smell, or taste.

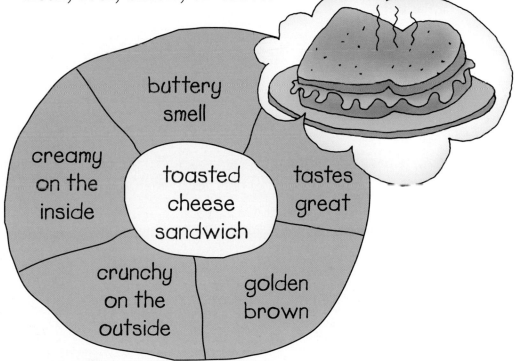

TIP This describing wheel goes with the paragraph on page 58.

Comparing Two Subjects

A **Venn diagram** helps you compare two subjects. It has three spaces to fill in.

In spaces 1 and 2, you show how two subjects are different. In space 3, you show how the subjects are alike.

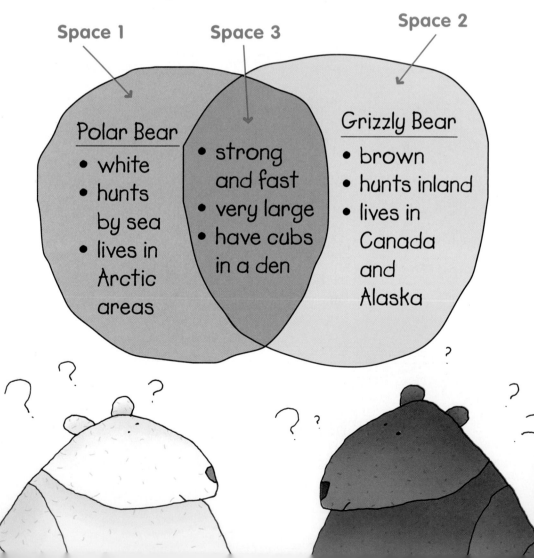

Space 1

Space 3

Space 2

Polar Bear
- white
- hunts by sea
- lives in Arctic areas

- strong and fast
- very large
- have cubs in a den

Grizzly Bear
- brown
- hunts inland
- lives in Canada and Alaska

Making a Story Map

A **story map** helps you remember the important parts of a story, in order. You can write words or draw pictures to help plan or recall the parts of the story.

Jack and the Beanstalk

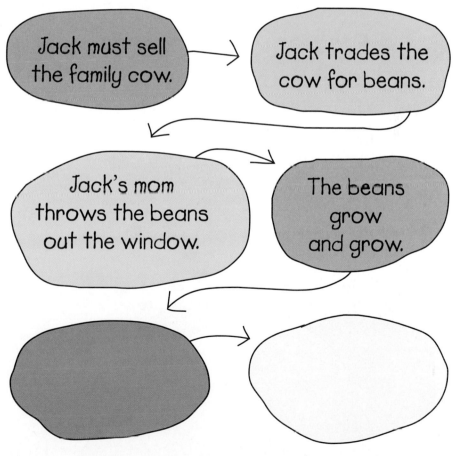

Jack must sell the family cow. → Jack trades the cow for beans.

Jack's mom throws the beans out the window. → The beans grow and grow.

Thinking Clearly

What bugs you? Do some classmates let the markers dry out? Do some kids forget to put their books away? Do you worry about missing the bus? These are little problems that you could try solving.

Got a Problem?

Thinking clearly can help you solve little problems and big ones, too. When you face a problem, just follow the four steps on the next page.

Solving a Problem

In this example, students try to solve a problem in their classroom.

1 **Name the Problem**

- Some kids don't put the caps back on the markers.

2 **List Ways to Solve the Problem**

- Make a sign that says, "Please, put caps back on markers."
- Have a student check the markers two times a day.

3 **Choose the Best Solution**

- Talk about the choices.
- Decide on the best plan.

4 **Put Your Plan into Action**

- If one plan doesn't work, try another.

Working in Groups

Everybody works in groups. Doctors and firefighters work in groups. Teachers and students do, too!

Teaming Up

Why do people work in groups? Groups can do big jobs. What must everybody in a group remember to do? Everybody must get along and try hard.

Planning TIPS

TALK about your assignment or job. Make sure everybody understands it.

SHARE your ideas. Take turns and listen carefully.

PLAN the work. Everybody should have a job to do.

PUT your plan on paper.

Group Plan

1. Job: We need to plan a birthday party.

2. When: The party will be at 2:00 p.m. Friday, Oct. 12.

3. Things to do:
   - Vijay and Tonya bring cookies.
   - Steve and Marcie make a banner.
   - Shavvon plans games.

Taking Tests

School keeps you busy. You read and write. Then practice new skills. You make things. Then you take tests!

Learning and Showing

Tests are not as much fun as some of the things you do, but they are important. This chapter helps you become a better test taker.

D.   Adjectives   Name   Tommy Sims

Fill in the circle before the word that best completes each sentence.

100%

1.   Of the three bikes, this one is the _____.
Ⓐ most fastest
Ⓑ faster
Ⓒ more faster
● fastest

Great Job, Tommy!

2.   A truck is _____ than a car.
Ⓐ big
Ⓑ m_____er
Ⓓ big

3.   _____puters are the _____ machines of all.
smarter
Ⓑ most smartest
● smartest
Ⓓ more smarter

Matching Test

A **matching** test has two lists of words. You must find the words from each list that go together.

- Study both lists very carefully.
- Then start with the first word in the left column. Try it with each word in the right column until you make a match.

Sample:

Making Compound Words

Directions: Draw a line between the words that make compound words.

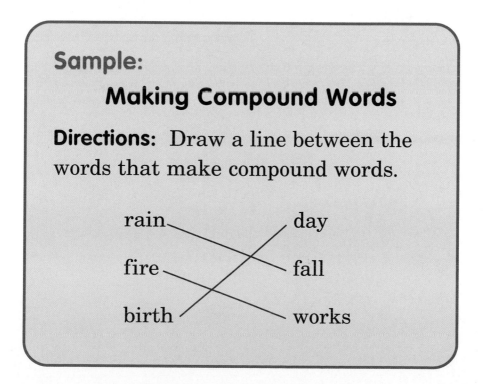

rain   day

fire   fall

birth   works

Multiple-Choice Test

A **multiple-choice** test may have a list of sentences to complete. You must pick the best choice to complete each sentence.

- Read the sentence with each choice.
- Then reread the sentence with your best choice. Be sure it makes sense.

Sample:

Farm Animals

Directions: Fill in the circle in front of the word that best completes each sentence.

1. A baby sheep is called a _____.

   ⓐ calf   🅑 lamb   ⓒ fawn

2. A group of sheep is called a _____.

   ⓐ fawn   ⓑ band   🅒 flock

Fill-in-the-Blanks Test

A **fill-in-the-blanks** test gives a list of sentences to complete. You must write the correct word or words in the blanks.

- Read each sentence very carefully.
- Count how many blanks you need to fill.
- Be sure your answer makes sense.

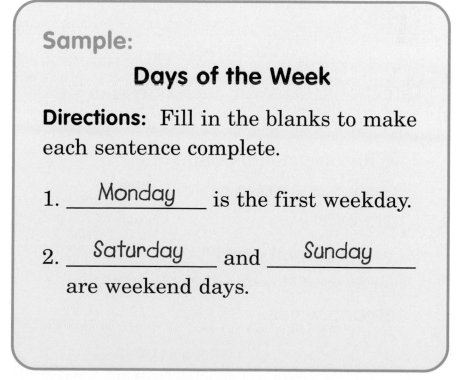

Sample:

Days of the Week

Directions: Fill in the blanks to make each sentence complete.

1. _____Monday_____ is the first weekday.

2. _____Saturday_____ and _____Sunday_____ are weekend days.

Short-Answer Test

A **short-answer** test gives questions to answer in complete sentences.

- Read the question.
- Think about your answer.
- Write your sentence. Use a few words from the question to begin your sentence.

Sample:

Weather

Directions: Answer each question in a complete sentence.

1. What are clouds made of?
   Clouds are made of tiny drops of water.

2. What is a blizzard?
   A blizzard is a snowstorm with strong winds.

Test-Taking TIPS

WRITE your name on your paper.

FOLLOW along as your teacher goes over the directions.

ASK questions if you do not understand something.

WRITE the answers you know.

SKIP the ones you're not sure of.

Then **GO BACK** to answer the ones you skipped.

Check to make sure you answered all the questions.

Proofreader's Guide

Using Punctuation

A "walk" signal tells you to go. A "don't walk" signal tells you to stop. These signals are very important.

Stopping and Going

Punctuation marks are signals you use in writing. For example, you use a period to signal a stop at the end of a sentence. You use a comma to signal a pause. You can learn about using punctuation in this chapter.

Use a Period

At the End of a Telling Sentence

George and Martha are silly.

After an Abbreviation

Mr. Plant

Ms. Blossom

Dr. Weed

Between Dollars and Cents

I have $2.25 in my pocket.

Use a Question Mark

After a Question
Who sat on my lunch?

Use an Exclamation Point

After an "Excited" Word
Wow! Awesome! Yuck!

After a Sentence That Shows Strong Feeling
There's a skunk on the playground!

Use a Comma

Between a City and a State
El Paso, Texas

Between the Day and the Year
July 4, 1776

After Introductory Words
When we race, J. J. likes to win.

A comma looks like a period with a tail on it (,).

After the Greeting in a Letter
Dear Grandpa,

After the Closing in a Letter
Love,
Liz

Between Words in a Series
I love red, purple, and silver.

To Keep Big Numbers Clear
My big brother is trying to save $10,000!

To Help Set Off a Speaker's Words
Ross said, "I love kickball!"

Use an Apostrophe

To Make a Contraction

Two Words	Contraction
do not	don't
we will	we'll
has not	hasn't
cannot	can't

To Show Ownership

my brother's frog
(One brother owns the frog.)

my two brothers' frog
(Two brothers own the frog.)

Use Underlining

For Titles of Books and Magazines

I read <u>The Mouse That Snored.</u>

Use Quotation Marks

Before and After a Speaker's Words

"I love carrots," said Sam,

For Titles of Stories and Poems

I called my story "Our New Pet."

Checking Mechanics

Rules help you in many ways. There are rules to help keep you safe. There are rules to help you play games. There are also rules to help you with your writing.

Rules for Writing

This chapter lists many rules for the **mechanics of writing**. You will learn about using capital letters, writing plurals, and much more. *Remember:* Rules will help you write!

Use Capital Letters

For the First Word in a Sentence
➚Fireflies light up the garden.

For a Speaker's First Word
Mr. Smith said, "Look at this
spiderweb." ➚

For Names and Titles
➚Jackie Wilson
Dr. Small

For the Word "I"
What will I say to him?
➚

Use Capital Letters

For Titles of Books, Stories, Poems, . . .

→ Aesop's Fox (book)

"Lost in the Woods" (story)

"Elephant for Sale" (poem)

Spider (magazine)

For Days, Months, and Holidays

→ Friday   January   Thanksgiving

For Names of Places

→ Canada   Rocky Mountains

Ohio   Main Street

Chicago   Sears Tower

For Plurals

Add "s" to make the plural of most nouns.

boy → boy**s**   wing → wing**s**

Add "es" to make the plural of nouns ending in *s, x, sh,* and *ch.*

glass → glass**es**   bush → bush**es**

Change the word to make the plural of some nouns.

child → **children**   man → **men**

Change the "y" to "i" and add "es" to nouns with a consonant before the *y.*

sky → sk**ies**   story → stor**ies**

Use Abbreviations

For Titles of People
Mister → Mr.   Doctor → Dr.

For Days of the Week
Sunday	Sun.	Thursday	Thurs.
Monday	Mon.	Friday	Fri.
Tuesday	Tues.	Saturday	Sat.
Wednesday	Wed.		

For Months of the Year
January	Jan.	July	Jul.
February	Feb.	August	Aug.
March	Mar.	September	Sept.
April	Apr.	October	Oct.
May	May	November	Nov.
June	Jun.	December	Dec.

Post Office Address Abbreviations
Avenue	AVE	Road	RD
Drive	DR	South	S
East	E	Street	ST
North	N	West	W

Post Office State Abbreviations

Alabama	AL		Montana	MT
Alaska	AK		Nebraska	NE
Arizona	AZ		Nevada	NV
Arkansas	AR		New Hampshire	NH
California	CA		New Jersey	NJ
Colorado	CO		New Mexico	NM
Connecticut	CT		New York	NY
Delaware	DE		North Carolina	NC
District of Columbia	DC		North Dakota	ND
Florida	FL		Ohio	OH
Georgia	GA		Oklahoma	OK
Hawaii	HI		Oregon	OR
Idaho	ID		Pennsylvania	PA
Illinois	IL		Rhode Island	RI
Indiana	IN		South Carolina	SC
Iowa	IA		South Dakota	SD
Kansas	KS		Tennessee	TN
Kentucky	KY		Texas	TX
Louisiana	LA		Utah	UT
Maine	ME		Vermont	VT
Maryland	MD		Virginia	VA
Massachusetts	MA		Washington	WA
Michigan	MI		West Virginia	WV
Minnesota	MN		Wisconsin	WI
Mississippi	MS		Wyoming	WY
Missouri	MO			

Checking Your Spelling

This spelling list is in ABC order. It includes many of the important words you will use in your writing. Check this list when you are not sure how to spell a word. (Also check a classroom dictionary for help.)

A

about
again
alone
animal
ant
are
ask
aunt
away

B

back
bad
bank
bed
been
before
believe
bell
best
big
black
blocks
blue
boat
bones
book
born
box
bricks
bright
broke

broom
brother
brown
burn
but
by

C

cake
call
candle
candy
cards
chicken
chicks
children
clean
clock
colors
comes
cookies
corner

could
crowded

D

daddy
dance
dark
desks
didn't
doesn't
dog
doll
dollars
done
don't
door
dream
drop
dropping
duck

E

each
eat
eggs
eight
eye

F

fall
farm
fast
feather
feel
fight
fire
five
floor
flowers
fly
flying

food
foot
for
forgot
fort
four
Friday
frog
front
full
fun
funny

G

game
give
going
good
grass
green

H

hair
half
hall
hand
happen
hard
has
head
help
hid
hidden
high
hill
hit
hook
hope
horse
hot
hours
how
hurt

I

I
ice
I'm
its
it's
I've

J

jam
jelly
just

K

keep
kids
kite
kitten
knew

L

lady
land
last
laugh
let
letter
licked
light
log
lonely
look
lot
loud
love

M

make
many
may
men

milk
Monday
money
monkey
month
moon
more
morning
most
mouse
move

N

name
need
new
next
nice
night
nine
not
now

O

okay
once
one
open
orange
other
ours

P

party
penny
play
please
poor
porch
post
pour
pretty
pull
purple

Q

quick
quiet

R

rabbit
rain
ready
really
ride
road
rode
room
rope

S

said
Saturday
says
school

seven
shoes
should
six
skies
sleep
socks
soft
something
soon
sound
stairs
stick
still
stopping
store
storm
street
summer
Sunday
sure
swimming
swing

T

take
teacher
teeth
tcll
ten
thank
their
there
they're
three
Thursday
told
tooth
train
tree
trucks
try
Tuesday
turkeys
turn
two

U

under
until
use

V

van
very

W

wall
water
weather
Wednesday
week
went
what
when
where
white

who
why
wish
women
won
wool
work
would

X

X ray

Y

year
yellow
your
you're

Z

zoo

Spelling TIPS

Make a SPELLING NOTEBOOK

Save one or two pages for each letter in the alphabet. Write **A** at the top of the **"A word"** pages, **B** at the top of the **"B word"** pages, and so on. When you find words that are hard, add them to your notebook.

Read over your notebook often. You will soon know how to spell the words.

Use a SPELLING PLAN

* Look at the word and say it.
* Spell it aloud.
* Say the word again, sound by sound. Notice the spelling of each sound.
* Cover the word and spell it on paper.
* Check the spelling.
* If you made a mistake, try again.

Learn Some
SPELLING TRICKS

For some words, you may make the same mistake over and over again. When this happens, try one of these tricks:

* Say the word aloud. Say the hard letters the loudest.

  Say **rabbit** like **rabBIT**.

* Spell the word on paper. Underline the hard letters, or print them bigger than the other letters.

* Think of a saying to help you remember a spelling:

  A bear is **hidDEN** in the **DEN**.

Using the Right Word

Some words sound alike, but they have different spellings. They also have different meanings. These words are called **homophones**.

ant   An **ant** crawled onto my finger.

aunt   My **aunt** likes to tell jokes.

ate   Liz **ate** lunch with me.

eight   I have **eight** crayons.

bare   My **bare** hands are freezing.

bear   Ira has a teddy **bear**.

blew   Dakota **blew** the biggest bubble.

blue   A robin's egg is **blue**.

dear   My grandma is a **dear** woman.

deer   The **deer** ran into the woods.

eye   Lu winks her **eye**.

I   **I** love to draw cats.

for   Miss Nelson made cookies **for** us.

four   Nick ate **four** tacos.

hear   I like to hear birds sing.

here   Who sits here?

its   The dog ate its food.

it's   I think it's about 8:00. (*it's* = it is)

knew   I knew my ABC's last year.

new   We have a new girl in our class.

know   Do you know her name?

no   Robert said, "No, I don't."

made   We made popcorn for a snack.

maid   Amelia Bedelia is a funny maid.

meat   Some people don't eat **meat**.

meet   I'll **meet** you at the clubhouse.

one   My baby brother is **one** year old.

won   Liz **won** a prize at the fair.

read   Mr. Lee **read** a funny poem.

red   I gave him a **red** apple.

road   Tony lives on a country **road**.

rode   He **rode** his bike to school.

sea   A **sea** is a big body of water.

see   Come and **see** my pet snake.

sew — My grandma likes to **sew** for me.

so — I'll hurry **so** we're not late.

son — My dad is the **son** of his dad.

sun — Plants need **sun** and water.

tail — A beaver has a flat **tail**.

tale — <u>Cinderella</u> is a fairy **tale**.

their — We used **their** bikes.
(*Their* shows ownership.)

there — **There** are four of them.

they're — **They're** mountain bikes.
(*they're* = they are)

to   I like to read funny books.

two   I read two joke books today.

too   Joe likes joke books, too.

wear   I like to wear floppy hats.

where   Where are you going?

wood   The fence is made of wood.

would   Dawn would like to go home.

your   What is your favorite video?

you're   You're a great singer.
(you're = you are)

Checking Your Sentences

What do I need to know?

A **sentence** tells a complete idea and has two parts.

1. The **subject** is the naming part.

2. The **verb** is the telling part. The verb tells what the subject is doing.

My <u>**mom**</u> <u>**rides**</u> a motorcycle.
 subject verb

A **sentence** begins with a capital letter. It ends with a period, a question mark, or an exclamation point.

→ Grandpa climbs trees. ←

Kinds of Sentences

A **telling sentence** (*declarative*) makes a statement.

Soccer is my favorite game.

An **asking sentence** (*interrogative*) asks a question.

Will you play with me?

A **commanding sentence** (*imperative*) makes a request or gives a command.

Kick with the side of your foot.

An **exciting sentence** (*exclamatory*) shows strong feelings.

Watch out for the ball!

Understanding Our Language

All of the words you use fit into eight groups. These groups are called the **parts of speech**.

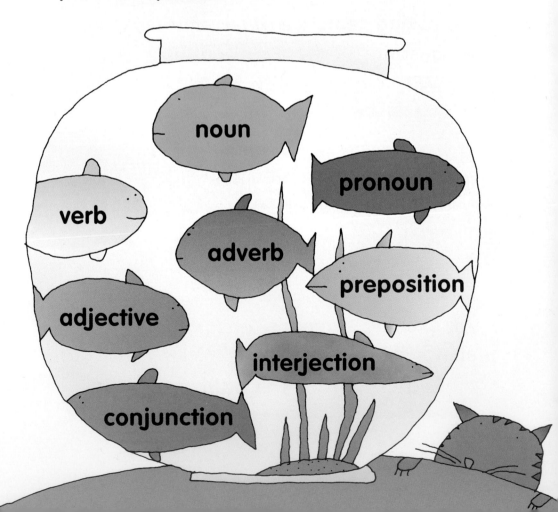

Nouns

What is a noun?

A **noun** is a word that names a person, place, or thing.

    girl   house   bike

Nouns can be **singular** or **plural**.

    singular: neighbor   house
    plural: neighbors   houses

Nouns can be **common** or **proper**.

    common: boy   street
    proper: Gus   Oak Street

A **possessive noun** shows ownership.

    Julie's flute
    the **boys'** tubas

Pronouns

What is a pronoun?

A **pronoun** is a word that takes the place of a noun. Here are some pronouns.

I	me	my	mine	he
him	his	she	her	hers
you	your	it	its	we
us	our	they	them	their

How are pronouns used?

Pronouns stand for nouns in sentences.

Holly played a game.

She hid the penny.

(*She* stands for *Holly*.)

Erik made cookies.

Then **he** ate **them**.

(*He* stands for *Erik*.

Them stands for *cookies*.)

Verbs
What is a verb?

A **verb** is a word that shows action or helps complete a thought (linking verb).

Spot **barks** at my neighbor. (action)

Mr. Wilson **is** so mad! (linking)

Some verbs tell what is happening now, or in the **present**.

Sarah **walks** her dog.

Some verbs tell what happened in the **past**.

Sarah **walked** her dog.

Some verbs tell what will happen in the **future**.

Sarah **will walk** her dog.

What are the different forms of past tense verbs?

Many verbs are **regular**. You can add *ed* to them.

   I **laugh**.

   I **laughed**.

   I **have laughed**.

    (with helping word)

Some verbs are **irregular**. You usually can't add *ed* to them. They change in different ways.

   I **eat**.

   I **ate**.

   I **have eaten**.

    (with helping word)

TIP See the list of irregular verbs on the next page.

Common Irregular Verbs

Present Tense	Past Tense	With Helping Word
am, is, are	was, were	been
begin	began	begun
break	broke	broken
catch	caught	caught
come	came	come
do	did	done
draw	drew	drawn
eat	ate	eaten
fall	fell	fallen
give	gave	given
go	went	gone
hide	hid	hidden, hid
know	knew	known
ride	rode	ridden
ring	rang	rung
run	ran	run
see	saw	seen
sing	sang, sung	sung
take	took	taken
throw	threw	thrown
write	wrote	written

Adjectives

What is an adjective?

An **adjective** is a word that describes a noun or pronoun.

> **Large** snakes live in the jungle.
> An anaconda is a **giant** one!

An **adjective** sometimes compares *two or more* nouns (or pronouns).

> An ant is **smaller** than an anaconda.
> An anteater is the **oddest** animal.

The words *a, an,* and *the* are **articles**.
Use *a* before a consonant sound:
> **a** parrot

Use *an* before a vowel sound:
> **an** otter

What are the other parts of speech?

An **adverb** is a word that describes a verb.

Erin ran **quickly**.   She fell **down**.

A **preposition** is used to help make a statement.

Maya laughed **at** the joke.

Joe sat **on** the beach.

A **conjunction** connects words or ideas.

I will dance **or** sing.

First I cried, **and** then I laughed.

An **interjection** shows excitement.

Wow! Did you see that bug?

Yuck! I hate creepy crawlers!

Using Theme Words

DAYS/MONTHS

Sunday Monday

Tuesday Wednesday

Thursday Friday Saturday

January February

March April May

June July August

September October

November December

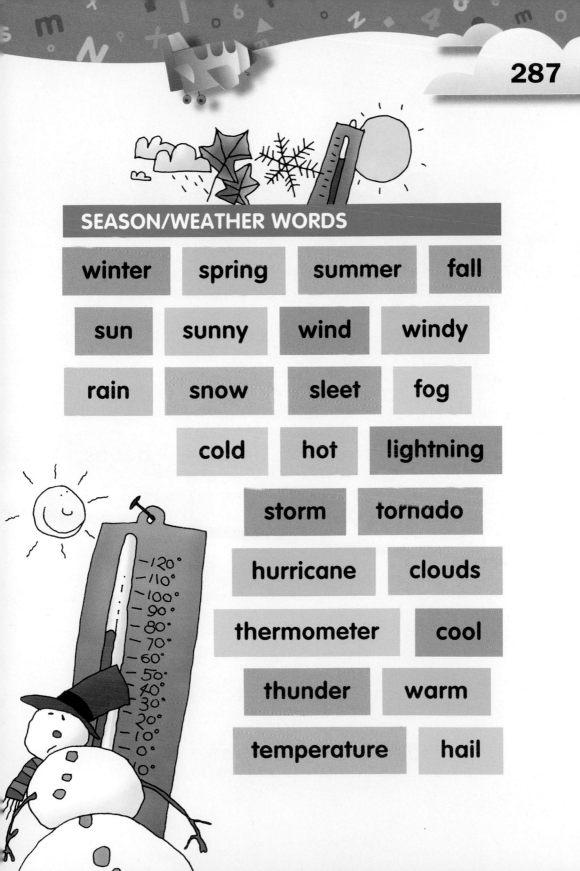

SEASON/WEATHER WORDS

winter   spring   summer   fall

sun   sunny   wind   windy

rain   snow   sleet   fog

cold   hot   lightning

storm   tornado

hurricane   clouds

thermometer   cool

thunder   warm

temperature   hail

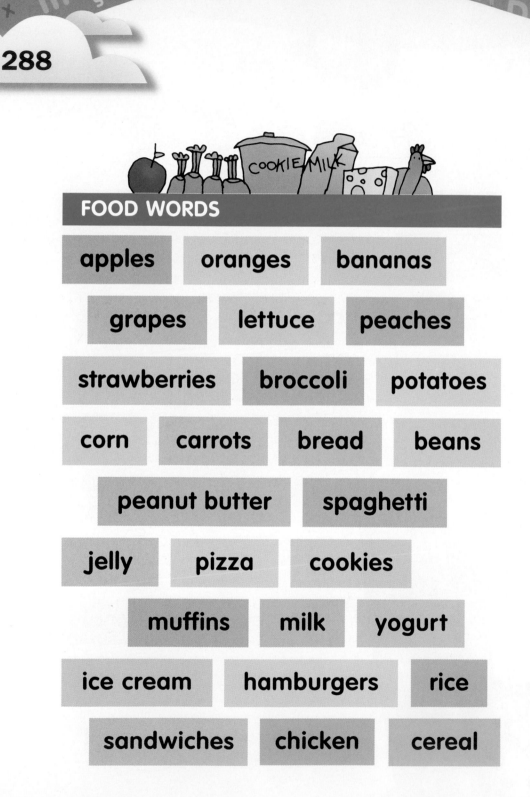

FOOD WORDS

apples   oranges   bananas

grapes   lettuce   peaches

strawberries   broccoli   potatoes

corn   carrots   bread   beans

peanut butter   spaghetti

jelly   pizza   cookies

muffins   milk   yogurt

ice cream   hamburgers   rice

sandwiches   chicken   cereal

COMMUNITY WORDS

apartment   town   city

house   police officer   doctor

mail carrier   shopping mall

drugstore   post office   church

street   movie theater   school

plumber   teacher   grocery store

hospital   librarian   nurse

neighborhood   gas station

garbage collector

Student Almanac

Using Language

The tables and charts in this section are about interesting language topics.

Sign Language

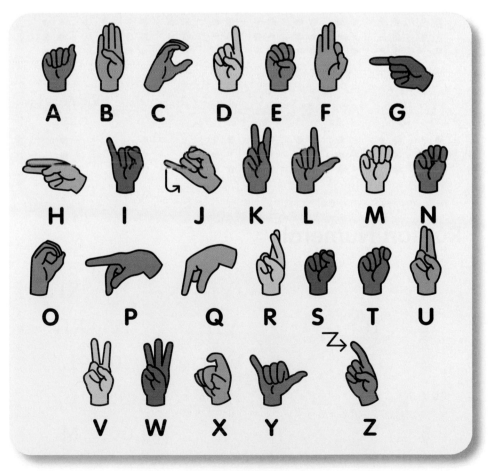

Braille Alphabet and Braille Numbers

a	b	c	d	e	f	g	h	i	j
1	2	3	4	5	6	7	8	9	0

k l m n o p q r s t

u v w x y z Capital Sign Numeral Sign

Roman Numerals

1	I	6	VI	11	XI
2	II	7	VII	12	XII
3	III	8	VIII	50	L
4	IV	9	IX	100	C
5	V	10	X	1,000	M

Saying Hello and Good-Bye

This table will help you say "hello" and "good-bye" in different languages.

Language	Hello or Good Day	Good-Bye
Chinese (Mandarin dialect)	dzău	dzàijyàn
Farsi (Iran)	salaam سلام	khoda hafez خدا حافظ
French	bonjour	au revoir
German	guten Tag	auf Wiedersehen
Hebrew	shalom	shalom
Spanish	hola	adiós
Swahili	Hu jambo	kwa heri
Swedish	god dag	adjö

Handwriting TIPS

SIT up straight when you write.

HOLD your pencil comfortably, not too tightly.

USE your best handwriting.

Handwriting Checklist

 Are my letters formed correctly?

✔ Do all my letters slant the same way?

✔ Do I have enough space between words?

✔ Do I like how my writing looks?

Manuscript Letters

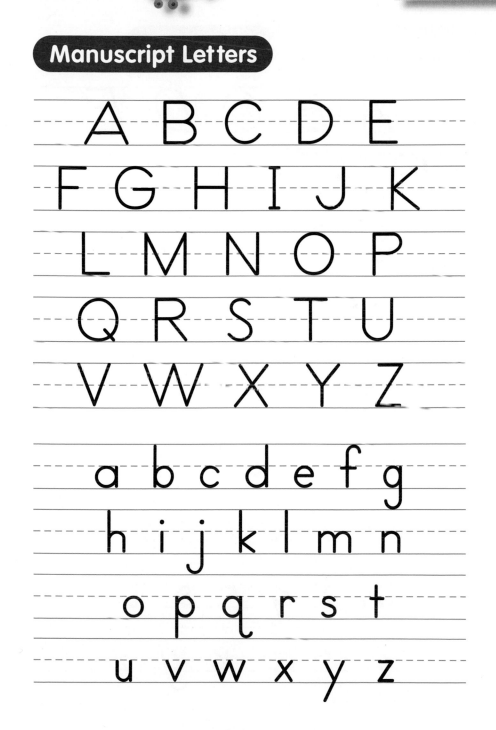

A B C D E
F G H I J K
L M N O P
Q R S T U
V W X Y Z

a b c d e f g
h i j k l m n
o p q r s t
u v w x y z

Continuous Stroke Alphabet

A B C D E

F G H I J K

L M N O P

Q R S T U

V W X Y Z

a b c d e f g

h i j k l m n

o p q r s t

u v w x y z

Cursive Alphabet

A B C D E
F G H I J K
L M N O
P Q R S T U
V W X Y Z

a b c d e f g
h i j k l m n
o p q r s t
u v w x y z

Exploring Science

The charts and lists in this chapter help you understand some of the wonders of science and nature.

Animal Facts

ANIMAL	YOUNG	GROUP	LIFE SPAN (YEARS)
Bear	Cub	Sleuth	18-20
Cat	Kitten	Clutter/Clowder	10-17
Chicken	Chick	Brood/Flock	7-8
Deer	Fawn	Herd	10-15
Dog	Pup	Pack/Kennel	10-12
Duck	Duckling	Brace/Herd	10
Elephant	Calf	Herd	30-60
Goat	Kid	Tribe/Herd	12
Goose	Gosling	Flock/Gaggle	25-30
Horse	Filly/Colt	Herd	20-30
Lion	Cub	Pride	10
Monkey	Boy/Girl	Band/Troop	12-15
Rabbit	Bunny	Nest/Warren	6-8
Sheep	Lamb	Flock/Drove	10-15
Whale	Calf	Gam/Pod/Herd	37

Animal Speeds

These speeds are for short distances. For example, a human could not run 28 miles in one hour. However, for a short time, someone could reach that speed.

MILES PER HOUR	1	10	20	30	40	50	60	70	80
Osprey (flies)									80
Cheetah								70	
Quarter Horse						47			
Coyote					43				
Ostrich (runs)					40				
Greyhound				39					
Giraffe				32					
White-tailed Deer			30						
Grizzly Bear			30						
Cat			30						
Human			28						
Elephant			25						
Snake		20							
Giant Tortoise	.17								
Snail		.03							

Measurements

Here are the basic units in the United States system of measurement.

Length (how far)

1 inch (in.) ——————← — one inch

1 foot (ft.) = **12 inches**

1 yard (yd.) = **3 feet** = **36 inches**

1 mile (mi.) = **1,760 yards** = **5,280 feet** = **63,360 inches**

Weight (how heavy)

1 ounce (oz.)

1 pound (lb.) = **16 ounces**

1 ton = **2,000 pounds** = **32,000 ounces**

Capacity (how much something can hold)

1 teaspoon (tsp.)

1 tablespoon (tbsp.) = **3 teaspoons**

1 cup (c.) = **16 tablespoons**

1 pint (pt.) = **2 cups**

1 quart (qt.) = **2 pints** = **4 cups**

1 gallon (gal.) = **4 quarts** = **8 pints** = **16 cups**

Metric System

Here are some common metric measures.

Length (how far)

one millimeter

1 millimeter (mm) .

10 millimeters

1 centimeter (cm) = **10 millimeters** _____

1 meter (m) = **100 centimeters** = **1,000 millimeters**

1 kilometer (km) = **1,000 meters** =
 100,000 centimeters = **1,000,000
millimeters**

Weight (how heavy)

1 gram (g)

1 kilogram (kg) = **1,000 grams**

Capacity (how much something can hold)

1 milliliter (ml)

1 liter (l) = **1,000 milliliters**

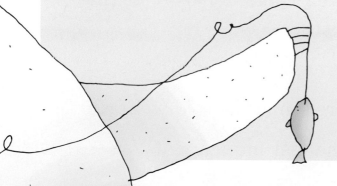

Our Solar System

The nine planets in our solar system orbit around the sun.

Mercury has the shortest year. It is 88 days long.

Venus spins the slowest. It takes 243 days to spin around once.

Earth supports life for plants, animals, and people.

Mars has less gravity than Earth. A 50-pound person would weigh about 19 pounds on Mars.

Jupiter is the largest planet. It is more than 10 times bigger than Earth.

Saturn has seven rings. It also has the most moons (23).

Uranus has the most rings (15).

Neptune is three times as cold as Earth.

Pluto is the smallest planet.

Sun

Mercury

Venus

Earth

Mars

Jupiter

Saturn

Uranus

Neptune

Pluto

Working with Math

You use math a lot. You add and subtract numbers, you count money, and you tell time. You also measure things, and so on.

From Adding to Telling Time

This chapter can help you become "math smart." The first part shows you how to solve word problems. The second part gives helpful math tables and charts.

Word Problems

Word problems are like little stories without endings. You make the endings by solving the problems! (Sometimes word problems are called story problems.)

Sample Word Problem

Suzanne has 2 bags of cookies. Each bag has 3 cookies inside. Suzanne's brother gives her another bag with 3 cookies inside. How many cookies does Suzanne have in all?

A word problem like this one is fun to solve. Find out how to do it on the next two pages.

Solving Word Problems

1 **Read the problem carefully.**
Look for important words such as "how many" and "in all."

> **How many cookies does**
> **Suzanne have in all?**

- If you don't understand part of the problem, ask for help.

2 **Decide what to do.**

- Do you have to add or subtract some numbers?

- Do you have to do two things—maybe add and then subtract?

3 **Do the problem.** Decide how you will solve the problem. You could draw pictures, use counters, or write a math problem.

Counters

● ● ● + ● ● ● + ● ● ● = 9

Math Problem

```
  3 cookies        6 cookies
+ 3 cookies      + 3 cookies
───────────      ───────────
  6 cookies        9 cookies
```

4 **Check your answer.**

● Start with your answer and work backward.

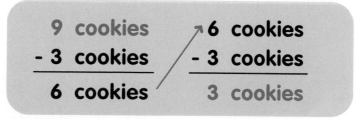

```
  9 cookies        6 cookies
- 3 cookies      - 3 cookies
───────────      ───────────
  6 cookies        3 cookies
```

● Try solving the problem a different way.

Addition and Subtraction Table

To add two numbers (4 + 7), find one of the numbers at the beginning of a row ⑦. Find your second number at the top of a column ④. Find your answer where the row and column meet: 4 + 7 = ⑪.

To subtract two numbers (11 - 4), locate the larger number in the table ⑪. Then subtract the number at the top of the column ④. Your answer will be in the row to the far left ⑦.

	1	2	3	④	5	6	7	8	9	10
1	2	3	4	5	6	7	8	9	10	11
2	3	4	5	6	7	8	9	10	11	12
3	4	5	6	7	8	9	10	11	12	13
4	5	6	7	8	9	10	11	12	13	14
5	6	7	8	9	10	11	12	13	14	15
6	7	8	9	10	11	12	13	14	15	16
⑦	8	9	10	⑪	12	13	14	15	16	17
8	9	10	11	12	13	14	15	16	17	18
9	10	11	12	13	14	15	16	17	18	19
10	11	12	13	14	15	16	17	18	19	20

Skip-Counting Table

2's	2	4	6	8	10	12	14	16
3's	3	6	9	12	15	18	21	24
4's	4	8	12	16	20	24	28	32
5's	5	10	15	20	25	30	35	40

Place-Value Chart

Here are the place values for 3,752:

3	,	7	5	2
thousands	,	hundreds	tens	ones

3 in the thousands' place is   **3,000**
7 in the hundreds' place is   **700**
5 in the tens' place is   **50**
2 in the ones' place is   **2**

GOOD POINT   You read this four-digit number as **three thousand seven hundred fifty-two**.

Writing Fractions

A **fraction** is a part of something. A fraction has a top number and a bottom number, like this example:

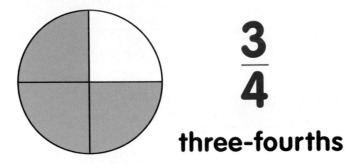

$$\frac{3}{4}$$

three-fourths

Reading Fractions

The bottom number (4) tells you that the circle is divided into four equal parts. The top number (3) tells you that three of the parts are being named. You read 3/4 as **three-fourths**.

More Examples

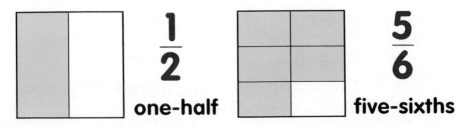

$$\frac{1}{2}$$

one-half

$$\frac{5}{6}$$

five-sixths

Counting Money

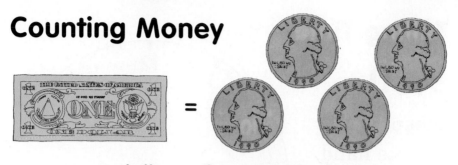

one dollar = four quarters

one quarter = two dimes + one nickel

one dime = two nickels

one nickel = five pennies

How much money?

If you counted all the money shown above, you would have two dollars and eighty cents. You would write $2.80.

Telling Time

9:30

When the
minute hand
is on 6, you
write 30 for
the minutes.

hour hand

minute hand

one hour = 60 minutes
one-half hour = 30 minutes

2:00

When the
minute hand
is on 12, you
write 00 for
the minutes.

3:25

When the minute hand is on a number, count by 5's from the top to tell the time (5, 10, 15, 20, **25**).

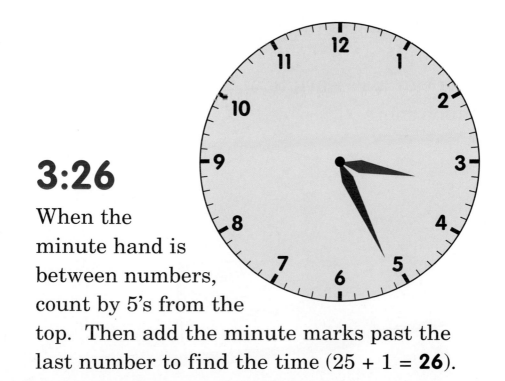

3:26

When the minute hand is between numbers, count by 5's from the top. Then add the minute marks past the last number to find the time (25 + 1 = **26**).

Learning About Maps

Maps help you in many ways. For example, a world map helps you locate other countries. A weather map can help you decide what you need to wear to school.

Around the World

The maps in this chapter help you learn about places in the world and in this country. You can also learn how to read maps, plus much more.

The Compass Rose

Most maps have a **compass rose** to show the four directions: north, south, east, and west. In fact, the compass rose is sometimes called the direction finder.

If a map does not have a compass rose, north is probably at the top of the page, and south is at the bottom. East is to the right of the page, and west is to the left.

Map Key and Symbols

The **key** is a list that explains the symbols used on a map. Symbols are like little signs that tell what is on a map. Here is the key for the map on page 319 in your handbook.

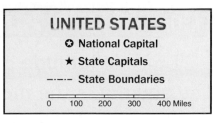

UNITED STATES
❂ National Capital
★ State Capitals
–·–·– State Boundaries
0   100   200   300   400 Miles

This key lists three **symbols**. There are symbols for the national capital (❂), for the state capitals (★), and for the state boundaries (–·–·–).

The Globe

The best map of the world is a globe. A **globe** shows the earth as it really is: round!

Equator

Prime Meridian

Lines of Latitude and Longitude

Lines of **latitude** go around the globe. The **equator** is the most famous line of latitude. It goes around the middle of the globe.

Lines of **longitude** go up and down, from the North Pole to the South Pole. The **prime meridian** is the most famous line of longitude. It passes through Greenwich, England.

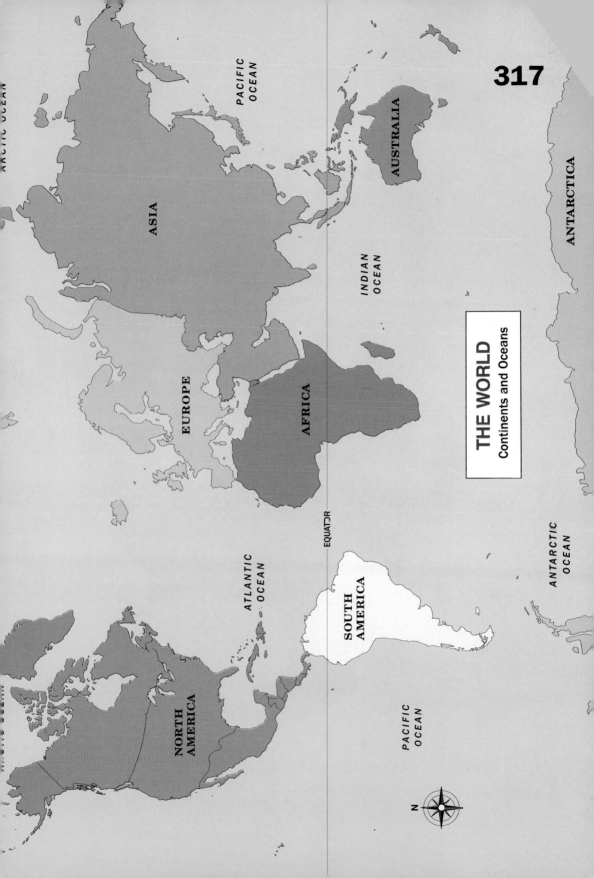

THE WORLD
Continents and Oceans

ARCTIC OCEAN

PACIFIC
OCEAN

ASIA

AUSTRALIA

ANTARCTICA

INDIAN
OCEAN

EUROPE

AFRICA

EQUATOR

ATLANTIC
OCEAN

SOUTH
AMERICA

ANTARCTIC
OCEAN

NORTH
AMERICA

PACIFIC
OCEAN

N

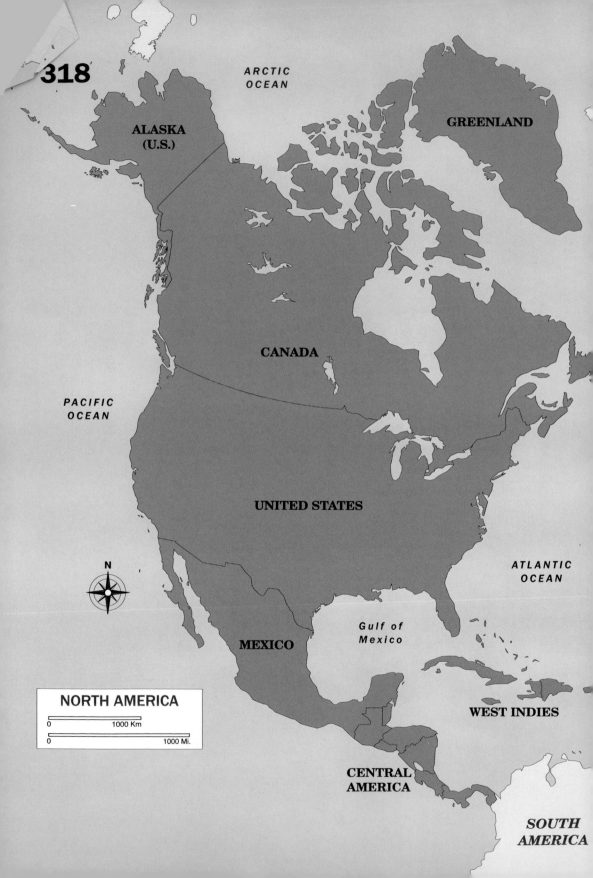

318

ARCTIC
OCEAN

ALASKA
(U.S.)

GREENLAND

CANADA

PACIFIC
OCEAN

UNITED STATES

ATLANTIC
OCEAN

N

MEXICO

Gulf of
Mexico

NORTH AMERICA

0   1000 Km

0   1000 Mi.

WEST INDIES

CENTRAL
AMERICA

SOUTH
AMERICA

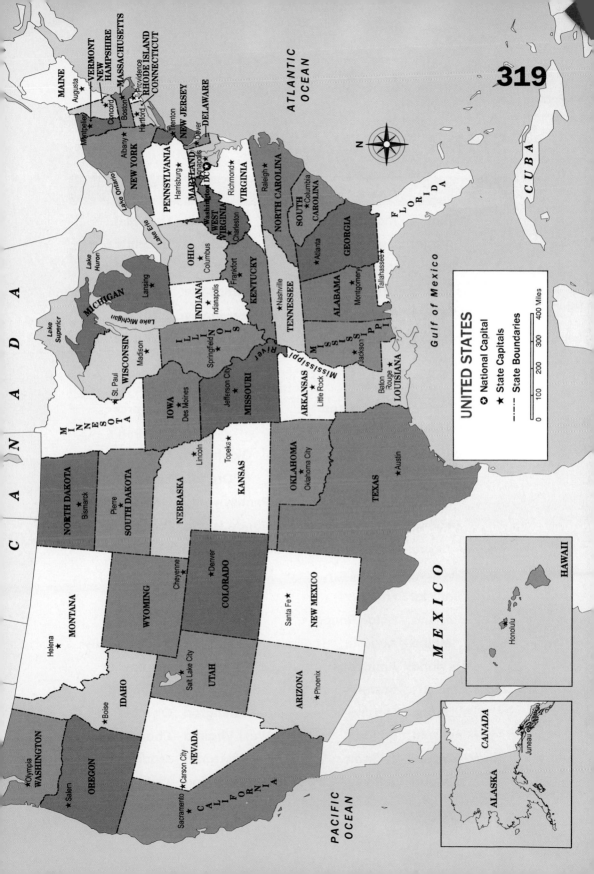

States and Capitals

State	Capital	State	Capital
Alabama	Montgomery	Montana	Helena
Alaska	Juneau	Nebraska	Lincoln
Arizona	Phoenix	Nevada	Carson City
Arkansas	Little Rock	New Hampshire	Concord
California	Sacramento	New Jersey	Trenton
Colorado	Denver	New Mexico	Santa Fe
Connecticut	Hartford	New York	Albany
Delaware	Dover	North Carolina	Raleigh
Florida	Tallahassee	North Dakota	Bismarck
Georgia	Atlanta	Ohio	Columbus
Hawaii	Honolulu	Oklahoma	Oklahoma City
Idaho	Boise	Oregon	Salem
Illinois	Springfield	Pennsylvania	Harrisburg
Indiana	Indianapolis	Rhode Island	Providence
Iowa	Des Moines	South Carolina	Columbia
Kansas	Topeka	South Dakota	Pierre
Kentucky	Frankfort	Tennessee	Nashville
Louisiana	Baton Rouge	Texas	Austin
Maine	Augusta	Utah	Salt Lake City
Maryland	Annapolis	Vermont	Montpelier
Massachusetts	Boston	Virginia	Richmond
Michigan	Lansing	Washington	Olympia
Minnesota	St. Paul	West Virginia	Charleston
Mississippi	Jackson	Wisconsin	Madison
Missouri	Jefferson City	Wyoming	Cheyenne

Facts About the United States

LARGEST STATE
Alaska   584,412 square miles

SMALLEST STATE
Rhode Island   1,214 square miles

LARGEST CITY
New York City   7,420,166 people

LONGEST RIVER
Mississippi River   2,340 miles long

LARGEST LAKE
Lake Superior   31,820 square miles

LARGEST DESERT
Mojave Desert in California
15,000 square miles

HIGHEST POINT
Mt. McKinley in Alaska
20,320 feet above sea level

LOWEST POINT
Death Valley in California
282 feet below sea level

Looking at History

When the Pilgrims arrived in 1620, there were many tribes of people (Native Americans) living in this land that is now the United States. These people had been living here for thousands of years. Each tribe had a way of life related to where it lived.

Native American Regions

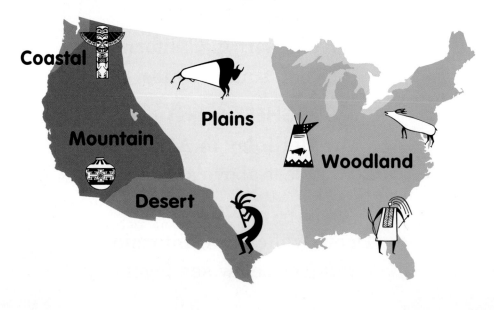

Coastal

Plains

Mountain

Desert

Woodland

U.S. History

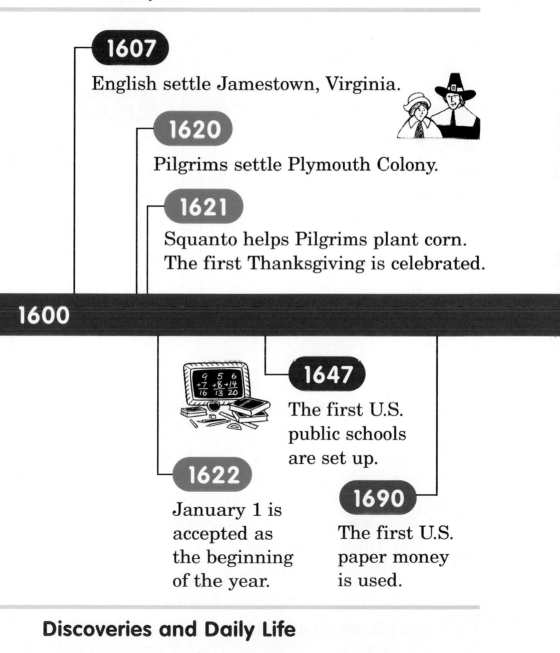

1607

English settle Jamestown, Virginia.

1620

Pilgrims settle Plymouth Colony.

1621

Squanto helps Pilgrims plant corn.
The first Thanksgiving is celebrated.

1600

1647

The first U.S. public schools are set up.

1622

January 1 is accepted as the beginning of the year.

1690

The first U.S. paper money is used.

Discoveries and Daily Life

U.S. History

1733

The 13 colonies are formed.

1731

Benjamin Franklin begins the first library.

1749

The U.S. population is close to 1,000,000.

1700

1736

The first American cookbook is written.

1742

Benjamin Franklin invents the Franklin stove.

1704

The first newspaper is written in Boston.

Discoveries and Daily Life

1750

Covered wagons begin carrying settlers west.

1789

George Washington is elected first president.

1776

The Declaration of Independence is signed.

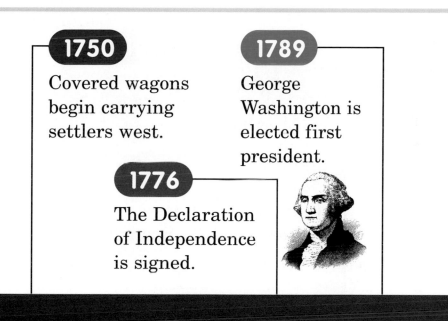

1752

Benjamin Franklin discovers electricity.

1782

The bald eagle becomes the U.S. symbol.

1786

The first ice-cream company is founded.

U.S. History

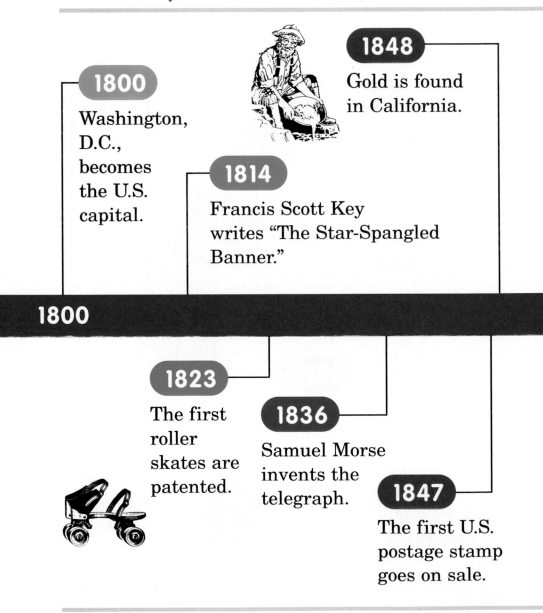

1800
Washington, D.C., becomes the U.S. capital.

1848
Gold is found in California.

1814
Francis Scott Key writes "The Star-Spangled Banner."

1800

1823
The first roller skates are patented.

1836
Samuel Morse invents the telegraph.

1847
The first U.S. postage stamp goes on sale.

Discoveries and Daily Life

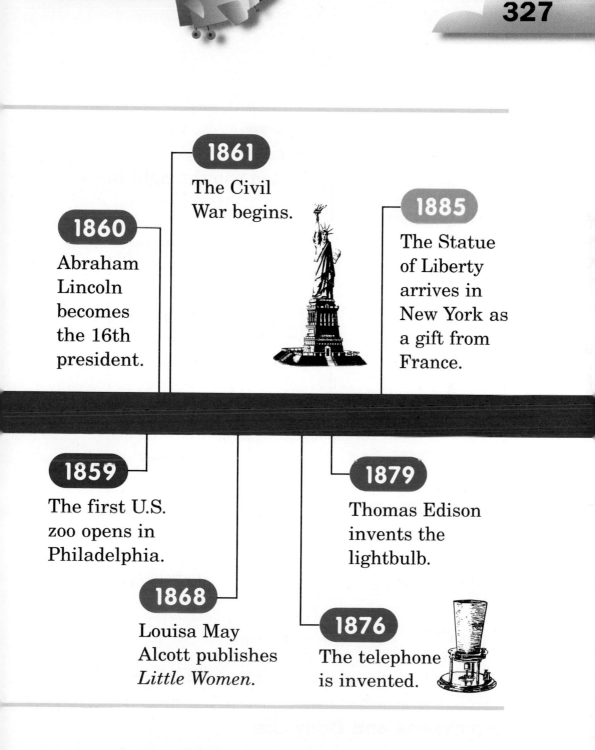

1861

The Civil War begins.

1885

The Statue of Liberty arrives in New York as a gift from France.

1860

Abraham Lincoln becomes the 16th president.

1859

The first U.S. zoo opens in Philadelphia.

1879

Thomas Edison invents the lightbulb.

1868

Louisa May Alcott publishes *Little Women*.

1876

The telephone is invented.

U.S. History

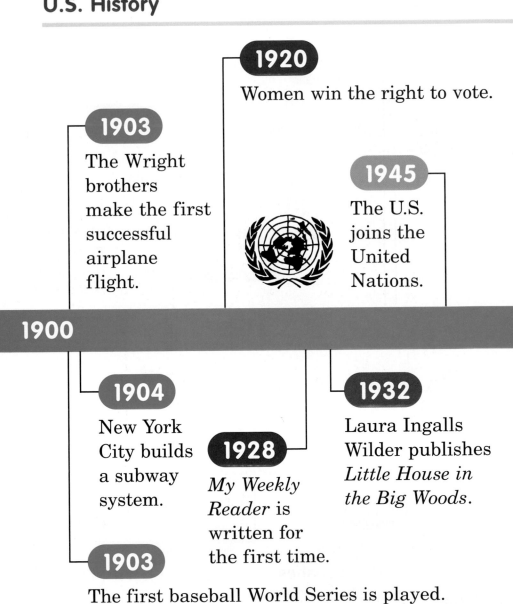

1920

Women win the right to vote.

1903

The Wright brothers make the first successful airplane flight.

1945

The U.S. joins the United Nations.

1900

1904

New York City builds a subway system.

1928

My Weekly Reader is written for the first time.

1932

Laura Ingalls Wilder publishes *Little House in the Big Woods*.

1903

The first baseball World Series is played.

Discoveries and Daily Life

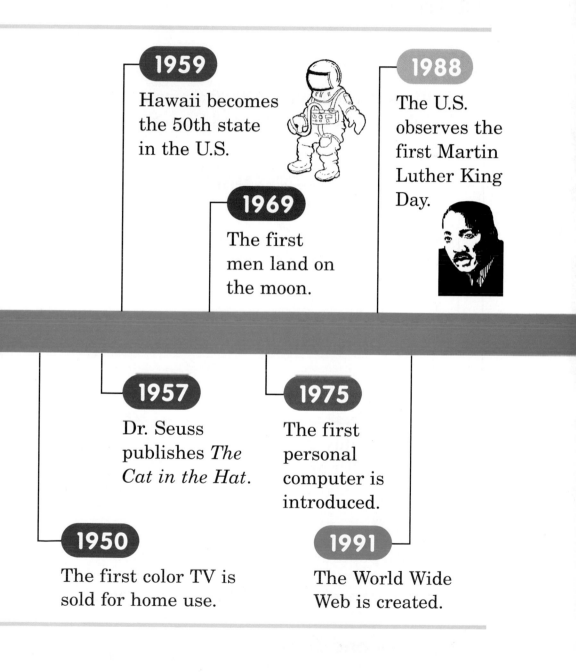

1959

Hawaii becomes the 50th state in the U.S.

1969

The first men land on the moon.

1988

The U.S. observes the first Martin Luther King Day.

1957

Dr. Seuss publishes *The Cat in the Hat*.

1975

The first personal computer is introduced.

1950

The first color TV is sold for home use.

1991

The World Wide Web is created.

U.S. History

2000

Wildfires burned over 7,000,000 acres of land in the western United States.

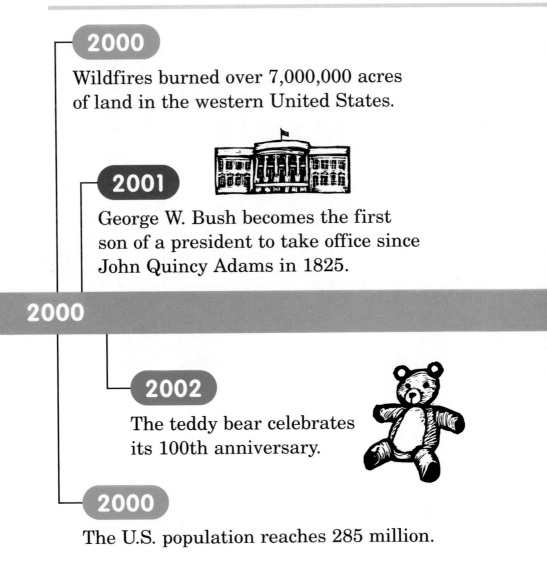

2001

George W. Bush becomes the first son of a president to take office since John Quincy Adams in 1825.

2000

2002

The teddy bear celebrates its 100th anniversary.

2000

The U.S. population reaches 285 million.

Discoveries and Daily Life

Index

The **index** helps you find information in your handbook. If you want to learn how to write a poem, you can look in the index under "poetry" for help.